*Manager's Guide
to Successful
Job Hunting*

ROBERT G. TRAXEL

Manager's Guide to Successful Job Hunting

McGRAW-HILL BOOK COMPANY
New York St. Louis San Francisco Auckland Bogotá
Düsseldorf Johannesburg London Madrid
Mexico Montreal New Delhi Panama
Paris São Paulo Singapore
Sydney Tokyo Toronto

Library of Congress Cataloging in Publication Data

Traxel, Robert G
  Manager's guide to successful job hunting.

  Includes index.
  1. Applications for positions.   2. Vocational
guidance.   3. Employment interviewing.   I. Title.
HF5383.T7   650′.14′024658   77-12038
ISBN 0-07-065096-9

1234567890 BPBP 7654321098

*The editors for this book were Robert A. Rosenbaum and Esther Gelatt,
the designer was Naomi Auerbach, and the production supervisor
was Teresa Leaden. It was set in Primer
by Black Dot, Inc.*

Printed and bound by The Book Press.

To my loving wife, Maureen

Contents

Preface

What it takes

This world is full of "how-to-do-it" books! Some of them, though, seem to leave out that all-important factor—the "how." Have the authors of these books really achieved their goals by using their own methods? Have they come up with any new or innovative ideas for their readers? Have they presented step-by-step guidelines?

In most cases, the answer to these questions is "no." The programs and concepts presented in this book, however, *will* produce results—but only if you're willing to invest a lot of time, effort, and work.

To write this book, I put myself on the job market and achieved considerable success by doing the things I tell you, the reader, to do. I've succeeded in carving my niche. I know what it's like because I've done it myself. I know that you need a strong shoulder to lean on, a knowledgeable hand to guide you along the right paths, and a commonsense approach that you can identify with. As you proceed, the successes you achieve will be *your own*, because you—not luck—made them happen. I trust you will find the answers to most of your concerns in this book.

Your future

It is my firm belief that the future holds tremendous promise and opportunities for all aspiring people. However, seeking out these opportunities and taking advantage of them require integrity, initiative, imagination, foresight, insight, and—last but not least—persistence, determination, and *hard work*!

While the future holds undreamed-of opportunities, it also holds undreamed-of competition. The days of "riding the gravy train," simply holding down a job, or marrying into success are fast disappearing.

Credentials

I've been in the employment agency business and the executive search business for a number of years. I'm currently the president of my own successful executive search and consulting firm. This book is meant to be a distillation of the many lessons I've learned while in both these fields and of the knowledge I've gained, firsthand, concerning the job hunt—seeking and securing the right "niche."

Being unemployed is depressing, lonely, and frustrating. Being underemployed is often worse. I've been in both situations a few times, and I sincerely hope that I can give you valuable insights into successfully creating the "right position"—your niche.

"Niche" defined

By this time, you may be wondering what I mean by the word "niche." Doesn't that word have negative connotations? Here are a couple of definitions for a start. By the time you're through reading this book, you'll have some definitions of your own because your niche—the right position for you—will be exactly what you want it to be, exactly what *you* make it!

The *American College Dictionary* defines a niche as "a place or position suitable or appropriate for a person or thing." My definition of a niche is as follows: "that single and exclusive position within an organization which, by definition and function, can be effectively occupied and retained by only one uniquely skilled and talented person."

You'll get what you deserve

I was motivated to write this book partly by my own firsthand knowledge of what it means to change jobs and partly by a careful study of a number of other books in this field, most of which, though well written and informative, simply don't deal with that all-important "how."

This book might not be the world's greatest literary masterpiece, but the programs outlined in it work—and work very effectively. However, *you* must take the time and effort to follow the programs and do the exercises I suggest.

As you proceed, you'll gain insight into the "how to" of identifying and creating the needs for your unique efforts, skills, talents, and abilities. Most important, *you'll gain an appreciation for yourself—your unique self.* Unless you accomplish this, all your efforts will have been wasted.

As is true of anything you do, you will get out of this effort exactly what you put into it. If you do the exercises in a haphazard manner, your results will be exactly what you deserve—no more and no less.

The reason for this book

The idea for this book occurred to me about a year ago when I was in a major city on the East Coast. What impressed me was the tremendous numbers of people whose faces reflected a certain "nothingness." After observing this nothingness for a number of days, the thought hit me: "Something is desperately wrong, and anyone who can do something about it could change a lot of lives."

I said to myself: "These people are truly unhappy. Why? Perhaps they lack purpose and interest in life. I'm just the opposite. I've never been happier or more optimistic. And why? Perhaps because I've found my niche."

That day, I swear I was the only person on the street wearing a smile. I wonder if everyone in that city wears the color that best matches their disposition, gray. Is this outlook, this color, reflected in your attire?

More questions

Why do people wait until they're either unemployed or miserable in their present jobs to change positions or improve their lot in life? Perhaps it's because the job-changing system is bad. Perhaps it's because they just don't want to take a good, hard look at themselves, recognize their successes and mistakes, and then take the necessary steps to change things. Perhaps they just don't know how.

Our job-changing system is fraught with frustration, disappointments, and indecision. It seems that everyone and everything associated with it is bent on promoting that frustration—from the newspaper want ads to the personnel managers to the employment agencies, and so on.

Why can't changing positions be something positive and ego-reinforcing? Why can't it be something you look forward to and not something you trust to chance or fate? Your search will be exactly what you want to make it. If you go out looking for success, you'll find it. If you go out expecting frustration and failure, that is what you'll find. *I sincerely feel that your job hunt can be one of the most rewarding and exciting experiences of your life.*

Grayness, nothingness? It doesn't have to be that way

During my years in the employment agency and search fields, I've seen many people who were unhappy and lost. Every once in awhile, though, I'd call on a winner, a person who was obviously a success. You knew from the moment you met that person that he or she was successful. Everything was just right—the appearance, the smile, the enthusiasm, the way that person walked and talked, and so on.

Now, a question: Why are people like this different from others? Perhaps they have found their niche. They are happy and at peace with themselves because they are contributing. They are solving problems and are respected for their efforts because they do their jobs in a truly outstanding manner. I guess you might say that such people are respected and happy because they are being themselves and are realizing some of their vast potential.

How about you?

How about you? Does the above description fit you? Are you true to yourself and to your career, or are you continually arguing and complaining about anything and everything? If so, perhaps the only person you're complaining about and are disappointed in is yourself. If that's the case, don't you think it's time for a change? And if you're going to make a change, why not make it a worthwhile one? Why not make up your mind to do it now? Your eight-to-five life doesn't have to be a drag!

A new approach

During my trips around the country, lecturing and giving work-shops for executives, I've learned some very useful lessons about them:

1. They rarely, if ever, see résumés or inquiries received unsolicited in the mail. (Somehow, these are always routed to the personnel department.) When they do look at such résumés or inquiries, they usually find that they are full of generalities and nonessential information. Most important, résumés lack "personality."
2. They're disappointed and turned off by the respondents to want ads.
3. They're looking for new methods—methods of reducing hiring errors and hiring costs and of involving candidates (potential applicants) and allowing their active participation (their prequalification) in the presentation and selection (prediction) process.
4. They're tired of being harassed by search firms and employment agencies, which have now reached the point of overkill and oversell.
5. Most important, they recognize that very few candidates can communicate who they are, what they can (and can't) do, what they want to do, and what and where they can specifically contribute.
6. They are concerned about the large amount of time, effort, and money needed to recruit, select, and hire the right person for each position. To make matters worse, they know that hiring errors can run to 33 percent.
7. Finally, they realize that only rarely will they find qualified and concerned people who are aggressively interested in their company and its products.

Shortly after that trip East, I became acquainted with a book entitled *What Color Is Your Parachute?*[1] This, in turn, led me to read other books, and the more I read, the more acutely I realized how poorly our entire population has been trained to utilize, happily and effectively, one of the most important parts of life itself—the hours between 8 A.M. and 5 P.M. How to plan your career and continue your career development—how to make a

---

[1]Richard N. Bolles, *What Color Is Your Parachute? A Practical Manual for Job-Hunters and Career-Changers*, rev. ed., Ten Speed Press, Berkeley, Calif., 1977.

position happen and create your own success—is something that few, if any, schools, colleges, or businesses teach.

Again I asked myself, "What is this mystique? Is getting a job that difficult?" I thought about what I'd been through in the past when I'd been out of a job. I came to recognize that the problems I faced were not unique to me; just about everyone faces them, and not only once, but probably several or many times during their professional lives.

The hunt begins

The books I researched all seemed, at the outset, to provide a good understanding of the situation. However, after reading a few chapters of *Parachute* I said, "This author is really making sense." But I had some further ideas about job-hunting books. The authors of most job-hunting books leave the explorations, the uncharted waters, the actual "how to" up to you and your initiative. Yes, I want you to use your initiative and your imagination as well. But I want you to do so in a very direct and knowledgeable manner. That's what you want too, isn't it?

Results

The results for the reader are the important and final determinant of an author's efforts. Again I ask, "Are most books in this field actually practical guides that assist the reader in what should be his or her continuing quest for a truly outstanding position?" The answer to this question is a resounding "No!" And so I have written this book, which contains a lot of answers and asks a lot of questions. My goal is to give you, the reader, a commonsense approach to job hunting and to carving your niche in a truly unique and professional manner—to making your success happen on a continuing basis. As someone once said, "There is no future in any job. The future lies in the person who holds the job."

Some words of caution

This book is for executives and aspiring management people. The techniques presented in these pages are extremely effective for people with business experience. Inexperienced people will court possible disaster with *some* of these techniques because they can—if used improperly or by the uninitiated and inexperienced—be intimidating and threatening to the interviewer. Entry-level positions for recent graduates from junior and community colleges, colleges, and universities must be handled somewhat differently, through different channels, and will be the subject of my next book.

One final word of caution. This book is directed solely at the serious, conscientious person who is determined to *make success and happiness happen now, and on a continuing basis,* and is not just hoping something will occur by luck, default, or happenstance. If you're looking for a job, just any job, you're wasting your time here. Put this book away and go directly to your nearest employment agency or newspaper—play their games. After you get burned enough, I'm confident that you'll be back to do it *right.*

Robert G. Traxel

Acknowledgments

Writing this book required a lot of love and effort on the part of a number of people. First, I want to credit and thank my dear wife Maureen, who loved, helped, and understood at "those trying times" and to whom I dedicate this effort. Next, I'll always be indebted to Mr. Frank Fiore, Jr., who taught me so much about the agency and search business and who helped immeasurably with the editing. Special thanks go to David Morgan for his encouragement and to Lewis Kasner, Gerry Gersovitz, Tom Kezar, Tryg Myhren, and many others who helped with research and ideas during the past four years.

Mission Viejo, California

Manager's Guide
to Successful
Job Hunting

ONE

Identifying the Problem

It hurts

Some of the worst emotional suffering you and your family will ever experience may come during the time, or times, when you no longer have a job. Suddenly and vividly you understand the meaning of the word "outcast." Your ego is damaged, and you're afraid to face the facts or make decisions—anything you do may make things worse.

Self-recrimination

You look at yourself in the mirror and say, "Well, here I am, all dressed up and nowhere to go." At first, it's shock, denial, and anger. Then comes the rationalization, "It's kind of nice having a little break. It will give me a chance to get caught up on all those things I've been putting off around the house."

But your children say, "Mommy, why is Daddy home? Is he sick?" Your wife looks at you and says, "What will I tell our neighbors? What are they going to think?" Your husband says, "Well, I guess that takes care of our hopes for a bigger home, a fine vacation."

If you are single, joblessness on top of loneliness puts you in double jeopardy. You've no one to turn to for advice and feedback, no one to lean upon. Your parents may say, "We've been working all our lives and have spent all our hard-earned money on you and your education, Now you can't even get a job." This may not be what they actually say, but you feel it *is* what they're thinking, and at this point you don't need their questions and concerns. You have enough of your own.

You need assistance, understanding, and—most important of all—knowledgeable support. Well, believe me, you can't and shouldn't count on getting it from anyone but yourself. This is going to be the time that you prove to yourself your real worth and what you're made of.

Step one from reality

Many people assume a position of total detachment from reality when they've lost a job or quit. They think, "Things will work out just fine. The word will get around that I'm available. All those contacts, friends, and so on—the people I've done so many favors for—they'll hear that I'm no longer with the company, and they'll come running. All I need to do is relax, sit near the phone, and pick and choose from all the offers."

Well, the reality of the situation dictates that *it's not going to happen.* In fact, in my many years in this industry, among the thousands of people I've worked with, I've never heard of this happening in a single case. What I'm trying to say, in the fashion of the commandments, is: *Thou shalt recognize that success must be made to happen* and *Thou shalt not procrastinate.* Success won't come searching for you—the kind of success that's truly worthwhile, that is.

Step two from reality

Enough sitting near the phone can lead to the next "usual step"—calling the competition or people you know, telling them that you might be available for the "right" opportunity. Either waiting or calling can result in discouragement and possible failure.

The "usual ways" may get you a job, yes. But the odds are very poor, and the kind of job you get might well jeopardize your future. Here's why:
1. You're bargaining from a position of weakness.
2. Your starting salary will be low.

3. The job is quite possibly not what you truly desire.

I'm sure you can see that the odds dictate: you'll be trading one bad situation for another, mediocrity for mediocrity. Yes, it may be a way out—a way of keeping the bill collector from the door. But you may be sacrificing the chance of your lifetime, the chance to find the "right" position, your own niche.

Allow this experience to make an indelible mark on your mind. In the future, remember the pain and anguish as well as the *loneliness*. Remember the despair of unemployment. Then, remember these very important commandments: *Thou shalt always cover thyself by being prepared* and *Thou shalt always bargain from a position of strength*. Above all, don't let your anger, depression, and hostility turn inward. Use that energy; turn it into aggressive and knowledgeable job-hunting efforts.

Rejoice, you may be one step ahead

So you think you have problems. Yes, you may. However, think of the poor people limping along in positions where they are underemployed or overemployed—not really contributing, simply existing—in the wrong slot. These people probably still have the agony of dismissal to go through. You're one step ahead of that game. You are taking the right steps toward achieving your immediate goal, toward finding "that new position." The fact that you're reading this book says a great deal about where you are. Let's look further.

Let's look at your problem in its proper perspective. Our definition of a problem, though simplistic, does "tell it like it is": A problem (challenge) is an opportunity looking for a solution. Your specific problem—unemployment, underemployment, a possible career change—results in disappointment, frustration, dismay, and self-recrimination (all because you're human).

Steps toward solution (what this book is all about)

1. Recognize and define the problem.
2. Break the problem into its individual parts—divide and conquer.
3. Plan and program the steps you will take to overcome the problem.
4. Assess alternative solutions to each part of the problem and establish goals.

    5. Choose the solutions that appeal most to you and to your common sense (gut feeling).

    6. Act on each solution.

Presto! Your problem is solved.

    OK, so that last job was a mistake. Make up your mind right now not to let the next one be *another mistake.*

Looking at your current situation

You can view your current situation in a very positive manner. Forget the negatives and *listen* to your innermost self. The answers may be right in front of you. The Bible says, "Ask and you will receive. Seek and you will find. Knock and it will be opened to you." These words have great significance in your situation.

It doesn't hurt to ask

You didn't find this book in the religious section of your bookstore, and you may feel that God and biblical quotations have no place in a professional book on a subject such as this. I'm hereby exercising my right to disagree. It is my firm opinion that a job or career change is one of the most important steps in life. You'll want to enlist all the help you can get. One source of help—the most important in my opinion—can be found in religion. I feel that it is right and proper to seek God's assistance and guidance in both good times and bad.

Danger signals

You're looking for a new position,[1] you're changing careers, you're concerned with your ongoing career development, and/or you're just plain unhappy. Why? Perhaps something isn't right, or a lot of things aren't right. Here are some danger signals to be aware of:

    1. You hate to get out of bed in the morning.

    2. You dread going to the office.

    3. You don't like yourself in this position.

    4. Your job is just a "job."

    5. Your efforts are continually unrewarded.

    6. Your attitude is coming through. (Peers in the office aren't

---

[1]Please remember that changing positions can mean moving up (with your present employer) or moving over (to a different employer). You must always look at your present employer's opportunities *before* considering others. The techniques provided in this book will help you to make that move—up or over—a successful one.

just giving you a rough time; you are, in fact, being ignored.)
7. You have no goals.
8. Your skills, for the most part, are wasting away with each passing day. You're feeling unfulfilled.
9. You don't like your boss.
10. Your philosophy and personality don't seem to match those of your employer and/or your peers.

These are just a few danger signals. I'm sure you can identify and add others. This is the recognition phase of problem solving.

Finding answers

How can you achieve the right solution, the way out of your current enigma? How do you find answers? By studying, gaining exposure, and listening—*listening* to your innermost thoughts. Through research you can arm yourself with knowledge, so that when solutions present themselves, you'll be able to recognize and exploit them knowledgeably.

Ask, but ask the right questions of the right people, and you *will* receive the answers. Seek, but seek intelligently and in the right places. Knock, but knock on the right doors and with the right amount of preparation—so that when a door is opened, you can take advantage of what is inside.

Problems, problems, problems

Problems are often signals (blessings) in disguise, sent to tell us, "Stop! You're not going in the right direction." If you ignore these signals and don't *listen, ask, and act*—if you simply take the easy way out (example, taking any job that comes along)—the only person you're hurting is yourself; the only future you're *limiting* is yours.

Learning about yourself takes time and effort. You're blind until you gain some insight into, and an appreciation of, your own skills, talents, and abilities. You're continually deafened by your surroundings. Listen to your inner self. If you take the time and effort to do this *you will never be disappointed or sorry!*

A word of caution

Listening to your innermost thoughts and feelings, listening to what really seems *right for you*, does *not* mean watching situation comedies on TV, playing cards, or drinking away your problems. Listening means working and studying—to gain exposure and knowledge, your ammunition—then relaxing and understanding what each effort and exercise (contained in this book and elsewhere) means to you and to your future.

The bigger the problem—and, let's face it, a job or career change *is* one of the biggest problems in life—the more careful study is required for an intelligent and knowledgeable solution. Don't fight the problem; solutions will make themselves known to you as opportunities.

Be honest with yourself and commit yourself wholeheartedly to the exploration and exploitation of each opportunity. Don't take just anything that happens to come along; don't lazily take the easy way out. The easy way will probably be a shortsighted solution that simply postpones the day and time you know is coming—the day when you have to look at yourself in the mirror and say, "Failed again. You didn't do it!" Once more you will have failed to go about carefully discovering what you're best suited for.

Heaven knows there are tremendous numbers of people out there postponing life itself—taking one simple job after another, wasting their skills and talents, and complaining all the time, but never making a sincere and honest effort to do something constructive about the problem. The time and effort you expend *now*, during your search—discovering skills, talents, and abilities—*is* well worth your while! Do it, don't postpone! The sooner you discover your unique skills, talents, and abilities, the sooner you'll be able to capitalize on them and exploit them and the sooner life will be right and fun for you.

Your goal

Discovering your niche in life, the great feeling of self-confidence that your position (not another "job") will provide you with—the opportunity to be yourself and make the most of your abilities, the opportunity to realize, almost totally, the potentials of your being—that's your goal. Once that niche is found, your eight to fourteen hours of work each day will become an opportunity to live life fully, to enjoy your own efforts and realize your goals, to utilize your skills, and to achieve recognition of your abilities.

So now it's up to you. Work the programs and work them knowledgeably. Listen to your inner thoughts and listen carefully. Plan your efforts, be honest with yourself, and commit yourself to yourself—to your future, to your goals, and to appreciating "who" you are. Remember. *you are the only person* in this world with your name, appearance, background abilities, and (most important of all) unique potential. And so, another commandment: *Love thyself!* Don't underestimate your value! Remember, you're all you've got. When the chips are down, the only person you can turn to is you. Furthermore, how can you expect others to love and appreciate you if you don't love and appreciate yourself?

This is an *action-oriented* program. The first step in any undertaking is the hardest step. You must realize that in this program, as in any undertaking, you will have successes and failures. These must be looked upon as learning experiences. The important thing is to get started and work diligently. There will be times of frustration and disappointment. I never said this would be easy. Your impatience will make each turndown or failure seem excruciating. You must remember that the Good Lord never closes a door unless he opens a window elsewhere. And so, your credo will be: *"Do it! Press on!"*

It's time to communicate

The first thing you must do is to be honest with your family and with yourself. Get the family together—before dinner. Turn off the radio and the TV. Tell your family that you're out of a job and that very little money will be coming in, which means that everyone will have to watch it financially, everywhere—and that each family member will have to help by:

1. Conserving on utilities
2. Cutting back on entertainment
3. Conserving on extra clothing

In short, everyone will have to conserve on everything.

Talk about the time element. Tell them you plan to work very hard at getting the best position possible, for you and for them—not just any job. Tell them that it's going to take a lot of time—probably two to four months—and that you're going to need their support and understanding. Open the meeting to questions and discussion. Then get yourself down to the unemployment office.

Get active and stay active

So now it's you, this book, and all the information with which you can possibly arm yourself—against the world. First of all, if you're going to run into domestic concerns, *get out of the house!* If this isn't possible, put a lock on that extra bedroom door. Set up a desk, have a phone put in, and make sure there are no distractions. (If you don't have a desk, rent one or use a table.)

It's really better, however, to get out of the house and do one of the following:

1. Go to the library. This is an excellent place to work, but there is no phone, and there will be some distractions.
2. Rent some temporary office space, perhaps from a friend. (If your friend is talkative, however, and the office is small, forget it. You're going out in a businesslike manner to make a position happen for you and only you. Don't introduce additional competition for your time and efforts.)

No matter which alternative you choose, remember to communicate your plans to your family. Keep them posted on what you're doing. Then get with the program and stay with it.

Now that you've taken care of your family and the environment, you must make some other arrangements:

1. Line up a secretarial service (if you can't type).
2. Line up a copying service.
3. Line up your research sources—books and industry contacts.[2]
4. Put an answering service on the phone or purchase an answering machine.
5. Locate your nearest full-service stockbrokerage firms. (Find the biggest ones—they'll have the resources to provide you with all the information you'll be needing. This will be explained in detail in Chapter 4.)
6. Locate your nearest library.
7. Consider using the excellent information available from the research departments of your largest banks.
8. Set up file folders, one for each company, and separate these according to industries. (As a maximum, choose five industries and five companies in each industry.)
9. Be sure to maintain your appearance: look and act the role of a professional.
10. Avoid wasting time on nonprofessional activities. Spend your time constructively putting your plan of action together—making it happen. Help your family to understand that they must continue to handle their fair share

[2]Don't include friends in this list. If you want to keep your friends as friends, don't go to them with your employment problems. You don't want someone to give you a job out of pity, do you? Commandment: *Thou shalt not include personal friends in business dealings.*

of household duties and responsibilities. You must continue to take care of your household responsibilities only before and after business hours. This is important. Remember that securing a new position is a full-time job!

Incidentally, if you still haven't been to the unemployment compensation office, go there right now. You've been paying for this insurance all your working life, and now it's time to collect. Pocket your pride and do it.

"I won't lower myself to that," you say. Again, remember that results are the important concern here. Having some money coming in will relieve some of the pressure. It *will* help. If you still won't do it, I have one last suggestion: Get a job. Yes, go out and get a job as a waiter or a waitress, a barmaid or a bartender, a telephone sales representative—anyting. Find a job that will provide you with a nominal amount of money for a few months (and one that you can hold down after business hours). Get something that will remind you just how much you had better keep your nose to that grindstone. Having such a job will also give you exposure (you'll be surprised at how much).

Self-doubt

Again and again, self-doubt will enter your mind. Remember that *this is a totally positive experience.* No one, but no one, wants someone who is filled with self-doubt who begs for a job. You must bargain from a position of strength, and so one of your first requirements is to get your act together in a positive way. You *are* someone special. At this point you probably don't believe that but, with the help of this book you're going to prove to yourself and the world that you are a very necessary and worthwhile person, perhaps an almost indispensable one.

"What I really need is a vacation"

Time after time, I've heard people say something like the following, and I'm sure you have too: "Dammit, I've worked for six years without a decent vacation. Now I'm going to take it. We've saved money, and we aren't hurting. So why not take a vacation now? It will clear my mind. I can *always* get a job when I get back." If you take a vacation now, you'll be accomplishing two things:

1. You'll be avoiding the problem—running away from it (or trying to).
2. You'll be giving yourself and your family a miserable vacation because you will all be worried sick.

Why not listen to your innerself? Listen to what your good common sense is saying to you:

> I've worked for six years without a decent vacation, but before I take one, I'm going to get another position—a better one. I'm going to carve a niche for myself so carefully that I'll be the best and only person in the world who can do the job. I'm going to choose the right industry and the right company, get a firm offer (with a starting date two weeks in advance), accept it, and sign the contract. Then I'll take a good vacation.
>
> Oh yes—I'm also going to see to it that the position provides me with enough money so that I'll be able to hire someone to do all those things I've been putting off around the house (and really didn't want to do anyway).

Perhaps, after you've found that niche, you just might decide to get right to work and let the vacation wait. Why? Because that position means more to you than any vacation could. Rather than wanting to get away from it all, you may want to "get with it," and as soon as possible.

Definitions

Let's look at some definitions so that we can be sure we're talking about the same things.

Unemployed

You shouldn't have too much trouble with this one. You're out of a job and have nothing to do but find another. Sure, you may be working, but you aren't making any money.

Underemployed

You have a problem or a group of problems. You have so much to offer—so many ideas, hopes, and dreams—but either you don't want to make waves by expressing all this, or you don't know how to go about finding a better position or making those opportunities happen in your present position.

Employed

You're doing your job. You're relatively happy, but are you truly doing your best? Are you realizing the potentials of your given skills and unique abilities? Is each day a challenge to you? Are you giving your all, but not moving forward? Yes, you're making money, but are you living for your time away from work and resigning yourself to nothingness or mediocrity? And if this is your feeling, just how valued are your services?

Just how vulnerable are you?

Perhaps a better question might be, "What would it take to replace you?" If the answer to that question is, "Exactly as much as it would *cost* to replace you" and if that cost is truly nominal— a three-line ad in the paper—you'd better watch out and get prepared. The next downturn in our economy might just be your undoing.

If you do the exercises contained in the following chapters and carry this whole effort through to its successful completion, you might well discover many skills, abilities, and talents you didn't realize you had. You might well recognize areas for contribution you hadn't thought of before. Your efforts will reveal new challenges and new opportunities which will help you to carve your niche in the company and industry of *your* choosing, whether you remain with your present employer or find another one.

The "right" position

There is no feeling in the world that compares with that of creating your own personal and professional security, making substantial and increasingly effective contributions, and being rewarded in direct relation to your performance. Let's look more closely at your ultimate goal. The position you want will:

1. Offer initial and ongoing communication and understanding
2. Allow you and your employer to develop a mutual feeling of confidence, appreciation, and respect
3. Reward you in direct relation to the effort you expend
4. Allow you to become (to some degree) financially independent
5. Make you feel "good" and "needed"
6. Afford you the opportunity to utilize fully your skills, talents, education, and abilities in the area where you can contribute most
7. Offer the right benefits and long-range opportunities and freedom to act within a broad structure
8. Be located in an area that is acceptable to you

9. Be with a company whose personality and philosophy are compatible with your own
10. Allow you to be the kind of manager you want to be

The time frame

How long is all this going to take? That's a wise, timely, and appropriate question. Experience has proved: optimistically, a minimum of four weeks; realistically, ten to fifteen weeks; pessimistically, who knows? It depends on you.

Yes, that *is* a lot of time, but your entire future is at stake. Spend this time intelligently *now*, and you won't have to waste it over and over again later in your career.

Why does it take that long? First, the personal and professional research efforts outlined in this book take time. You also have to make your contacts—gain the necessary exposure—and this takes time too. Then your chosen companies have to consider you and the feasibility of your proposals and program. All in all, a lot of time is involved, so plan accordingly and set your goals with this time frame in mind—ten to fifteen weeks. Remember, Rome wasn't built in a day.

If that seems like too much time because you're under financial pressure, this should give you additional inspiration to get out and do the job. You might call it the "inspiration of desperation." Remember, though, that if you go to the newspapers, the employment agencies, or the search firms:

1. There will be just about the same time factor. (You will be depending on someone else, and you know what past experience has proved in that regard.)
2. You will be giving someone else partial control over your future. Do you really want that?
3. You will be letting other people help carve your niche. What if they do a sloppy job?
4. You will be eliminating a substantial number of companies that don't work with search firms or pay agency fees or that recognize the limitations of newspaper ads.

Suppose you end up making another mistake?

TWO

Let's Get with It!

I'd like to recommend that you do yourself a favor. Put this book down, go directly to the nearest bookstore or library, and buy or check out a copy of *What Color Is Your Parachute?*[1] by Richard N. Bolles. That's right, do it now. Then read the book, and read it thoroughly. I am asking you to do this, because I don't want to quote Mr. Bolles at great length or have this chapter or the next several chapters balloon into a long book review.

Parachute[2] is a fine work. Mr. Bolles must have spent years gathering the invaluable information contained in the first six chapters. Like Mr. Bolles, I've spent years learning about and researching the problem of how to get a job. My experience has been firsthand. I promise you that many of Mr. Bolles's comments are not only true but also understated.

As you have learned from your reading of *Parachute:*[3]

    1. Your initial approach to job hunting is very similar to the approach that millions of unemployed people and tens of

---

[1]Richard N. Bolles, *What Color Is Your Parachute? A Practical Manual for Job-Hunters and Career-Changers*, rev. ed., Ten Speed Press, Berkeley, Calif., 1977.
  [2]Ibid.
  [3]Ibid.

millions of underemployed people take. Obviously, it isn't very effective.

2. Employment agencies, search firms, newspaper ads, and so on play the numbers game.[4] Are you a number, or are you a person—a potentially valuable contributor?
3. Yes, there is a creative minority among these firms and agencies. *If you're lucky enough to find them, however, can they and will they do the job with and for you?* Wouldn't you be better off doing it yourself? Wouldn't you save time and money and spare yourself false hopes?
4. You really don't need anyone else. You have yourself. The sooner you get down to work and start depending on yourself and believing in yourself, the better off you'll be.

Remember that you must concentrate your time and effort in those areas in which your chances for reward are greatest. In essence, you're out to acquire ammunition. And your ammunition in this job-hunting effort is *knowledge.*

Dispensing with the unnecessary

Less than 5% of the jobs paying more than $600 a month are filled through employment agencies. More than 80% are filled through:

1. The recommendations of friends already employed by the concern or
2. Through contacts, "Uncle Joe is a friend of the boss," or
3. Through tips that so and so is in need of a willing worker.

The remaining 15% or so of jobs are filled by responses to "help wanted" ads or through letters of application sent to firms with whom the applicant hopes to be associated.[5]

As you have gathered from *Parachute*[6] and from the above quotation, you must appreciate the importance of emphasizing the area where your efforts will have the greatest chance of being rewarded—where the odds are in your favor. It's called "referral." So let's dispose of those endeavors which have proved, for the most part, to be ineffective. You really have little or no need for

---

[4]Frequently, search firms, counseling firms, and employment agencies are staffed by people who, for the most part, have virtually no experience or expertise in the particular industry or profession in which they are attempting to place job hunters.

[5]Bernard Haldane, *How to Make a Habit of Success*, Acropolis Books, Washington, revised edition, 1975.

[6]Bolles, op. cit.

counseling firms, newspaper ads, employment agencies, or search firms. Let's take a look at "blind ads" (box-number ads).[7]

"Blind ads"

You might be interested in learning about some of the games that are being played not only with your head but quite possibly also with your future. Here are a few examples.

"Where are the unhappy people" game

A very cruel game is being played by a number of unethical people who place blind ads for positions a bit higher than the ones they have. Strangely enough, a person who responds to such an ad often finds that his or her present employer is contacted by the person who placed the ad. Perhaps this person calls the company or division president and says something like the following:

> "I have it on good authority that a certain person in your _____ department is unhappy in his present position. I'm very interested in that kind of job and would like to meet with either you or the head of that department to discuss where I might be able to. . . . "

Ouch! Incidentally, certain unethical agencies and search firms use this ploy as well.

And another

Sometimes a company's management will place an ad in the paper to determine how "loyal" the present executives are. You can easily figure out the rest.

What I'm saying is that, in all too many cases, responding to a blind ad isn't only a waste of your valuable time—it might also be suicide. In general, you should ignore most of the want ads and all the blind ads in newspapers and trade magazines.

I've got to admit that there are some things to be learned such as:

1. There is one chance in a thousand (maybe worse) that you'll happen on the position you want with the company

---

[7]Knowledgeable and experienced industry people frequently look upon want ads as a device used by the uninitiated and uninformed and as being a cheap method of attracting talent. If a company takes this attitude now, where will you be when it comes time for your salary negotiation?. Additionally, how much respect will the company have for you if you have been introduced through a want ad?

you want. If that's the case, respond with your background and interests.

2. You will learn about the kinds of jobs you *don't want* and the salary levels that go along with them.
3. You might find a part-time job to tide you over while you're seeking the right position.
4. You will have a chance to compare salary levels and perquisites.

Employment agencies and search firms

One of the best agencies used to figure that if it placed one person in a hundred of those coming through the door, it was doing quite well. Some odds?

Search firms honestly don't need you. They are recruiters; that is, they work only on specific assignments and (for the most part) only with currently employed people.

Search firms and agencies aren't all bad, however. In fact, they serve a definite need (remember that our efforts here are concerned with self-placement). If and when a recruiter calls you, *listen very carefully*—opportunity doesn't knock often. Furthermore, consider it a compliment to have been contacted. Then follow up with the suggestions and programs presented in this book. Make certain, however, that you carefully determine the credentials of these firms and agencies.

If you honestly feel that you need these people, I urge you to *put this book away.* This book requires guts (intestinal fortitude) and a dependence on one person—you. If you make up your mind to be the master of your own fate, you will have come a long way toward realizing that:

1. You can do anything you want to do.
2. You can be anything you want to be.
3. You can make yourself a success!

Let's start at the beginning

The "experts" have helped us eliminate a number of ineffective services. Now let's eliminate some things ourselves. Let's recognize and dispense with those "attendant aids" which history and millions of wasted hours have *proved* to be ineffective.

You must eliminate, along with the agencies, want ads, and search firms, the following:

1. The personnel manager
2. The personnel department
3. The résumé (and all its accompanying evils)
4. Introductory employment interviews (screening interviews)
5. The employment application form

Dispensing with the unnecessary: the personnel manager

The position of personnel manager is one with administrative duties, but few responsibilities in employment, and little authority. How does this relate to you and your position search? It doesn't relate, *because the personnel manager doesn't have hiring authority or responsibility.* So why are you wasting your time and effort with someone who cannot make decisions?

How did this position evolve and what is its reason for being? Someone has to take care of the following:

1. Paper shuffling
2. Answering phone calls from search firms and agencies
3. Writing ads and answering applicants
4. Wage and salary negotiations (perhaps)
5. EEO activities
6. Union negotiations
7. Other necessary details

The personnel manager is known in industry by a variety of names and titles. Some of these are:

1. Vice President, Industrial Relations
2. Vice President, Personnel
3. Personnel Manager
4. Manager, Manpower Development
5. Manager, Employee Relations
6. Manager, Employment
7. Director, Personnel

"A rose by any other name . . . " A personnel manager by any other name, or title, is still a personnel manager. These people, in just about any organization, are there to serve a function: to keep job seekers from "bothering" company management. Is this the kind of person you want to have representing you and your qualifications to the decision maker? Is this the person to whom you are entrusting your entire future with this company and in this industry? Is this the person you'll be asking to sell "you," your qualifications, and your unique abilities? I've always felt that when you want something tremendously important done right, you must do it yourself!

Moreover, personnel people will often admit that truly outstanding talent finds some way to attract management's attention. Top talent doesn't work through personnel departments. Enough said?

Dispensing with the unnecessary: the résumé

Somehow, the idea of a résumé never sat right with me. How about you? Did you ever like to write one? I feel that the best place for a résumé is next to you on the day you're buried. Why? Because it tells of your past.

Of course, some résumés make a feeble attempt to "tell it like it is." They may include a section on "position desired." This is probably the only part of a résumé that you feel good about. However, agencies and search firms tell you to drop even this because it "tends to limit your marketability."

Now comes the commonsense part: Why not carry this—"position desired"—right on through to an intelligent conclusion? Furthermore, why not expand on it? (We'll do this in Chapter 12.) What you want to talk about is your future—your plans and goals, your hopes and dreams. You want to talk about who you are, what you can do, and what you feel down deep inside that you can become, if only you can *make that opportunity happen.* That's what the rest of this book is all about.

Getting back to the résumé, what can you ever say on a résumé that isn't covered on a company application for employment? Furthermore, even after you have gone to all the trouble of putting a résumé together, you know that the person who reads it is going to ask you to fill out an application anyway—that is, if you can even *get* someone to read it. So, what is the purpose of it?

"Well," you say, "the résumé is meant to do one important thing—to get my foot in the door." Yes, but does it? That is what all the "experts"—the agencies, the search firms, and the counseling firms—are supposed to do. That is truly their only actual reason for being: to help you get your foot in the door or, to use their terminology, "to give exposure to qualified candidates."

Dispensing with the unnecessary: the employment application

The employment application is another unnecessary evil—just some more red tape. Let's look at it carefully. Once you've filled it out, just who is going to read it? And when and if someone does read it, will this person really appreciate all the effort you've put into it? Probably not.

You may spend as long as five hours on an application form, only to have someone glance at it for five minutes. Then it's tucked away in a file drawer, probably never to see daylight again. Not only is it a complete waste of your time and effort but, most important, it doesn't give you a chance to say what you can do for a potential employer or to indicate that your personality and that of the employer will match.

This is the twentieth century, and the résumé and the employment application are antiquated horse-and-buggy concepts. They shouldn't be part of one of the most important aspects of our business and personal lives—selecting the finest talent available for the development and growth of our industries and companies.

Now obviously, if you do away with the résumé, there is no need to write a "personalized" covering letter to send to each company, nor will you have to send a separate "marketing" letter regarding your abilities and your past accomplishments. You needn't spend your valuable time and money on methods which millions of others have found to be incredibly wasteful and irrelevant.

Fight city hall?

You say that you've been in touch with a few potential employers and that they've requested some information. I'm not saying that you shouldn't send them anything. That would be a bit out of line. What I'm saying is this: be as cooperative as possible, but do it right. Do a first-class job.

However, there is a lot of work and preparation to be done before you send anything to anyone. What you'll be sending or delivering personally will be explained in detail in Chapters 9 and 12.

Dispensing with the unnecessary: the screening interview

How do you feel during an introductory employment interview? Like a piece of merchandise up for sale or like a lamb being led to slaughter?

I feel that the screening interview is an artificial situation both for you and the interviewer. How can you be yourself during an interrogation? How do you think the interviewer feels?

Furthermore, what are the chances that an interviewer who

has seen six, eight, or even ten people that day will even remember you? Don't subject yourself to this pain, anguish, and suffering. Let other people do it—not you!

Where do we go from here?

Now that we've disposed of just about everyone and everything relating to the "old methods" of getting a job, what tools do we have left to work with? A short and very generalized listing might include:

1. You, with all your positive qualifications (and some that aren't so positive)
2. Your unique personality
3. Your common sense and logic
4. Your self-confidence and your attitude
5. Your knowledge, skills, abilities, and experience
6. Your unique potential to contribute to the company and industry of your choosing
7. This book

Do you honestly need any more?

Now it's a matter of researching, creating a marketing plan, following through, and helping your employer-to-be buy the benefits you can provide—in a logical, professional, and common-sense manner. The techniques I've developed for doing this can bring you the success you want, *but only if you make it happen.* Now it's on to the meat and potatoes.

THREE

The Product: All about You

The goal of this chapter is very simple: research, identification, and development of the product—you. Or, another way of saying this: to help you research, identify, reinforce, and develop your self-confidence; to make sure you recognize that happiness and success begin with one person—you; and to instill a strong belief in, and an appreciation for, the unique you.

"All right," you say, "I've got a lot of self-confidence." Great! All too many others will say, "I really lack self-confidence." Either way, the self-confidence I'm talking about is centered around this commandment: *Know thyself, love thyself!*

Whether you think you have self-confidence or lack it, the secure self-confidence I'm speaking about is based on facts. The facts that reinforce your positive feelings toward yourself will be acquired as a result of your written efforts in this chapter. Unless you are prepared with a pad of paper, pens, and pencils and with the time and environment to do some serious work—unless you're prepared to get down to the library and use it—do not proceed any further!

I've done a lot of talking so far; now let's get to work.

I dare you to be yourself

A lot of people go through life disliking—yes, even hating—themselves. How much? Well, just look at the alcoholics, drug addicts, and suicides. If you think about how such people behave, you'll realize how much they dislike themselves. People who like themselves take care of themselves. They recognize that life is short—too short to spend it being miserable and unfulfilled.

In other words, you have a choice! The pages of history are filled with stories of people who have succeeded in spite of all odds, physical and otherwise, in sports, politics, business, war—you name it. What kind of odds are you fighting? Chances are those odds are concerned with your poor self-perception.

For every person who has made it to the top in the business world on the basis of physical appearance or knowing the "right" people, there are probably 10,000 who have succeeded because of ability—proved ability. And ability, if exercised properly, improves with age, not like physical appearance.

A great deal of "if-ing" in life is concerned with physical appearance. This concern with looks is fostered by a continued bombardment of advertisements for health and beauty aids. These do have their place, of course, and if you're really ugly, there is always plastic surgery. However, if you are reasonably attractive, then a careful reading of Maxwell Maltz's book entitled *Psycho-Cybernetics*[1] will make you realize that you must concentrate on what's truly important—*what's inside you.*

To imitate or not to imitate—that is the question

Do you ever get the impression that everyone goes through life imitating everyone else? When you're young, Mom and Day say (sometimes in utter dismay), "Why can't you be like Johnny?" "He never acts like that!" As you grow up, you see the high school heroes—the winners—and wonder why you can't be like them. Then the wishing turns into imitation and into excuses: "If only I was like them, I could really be something."

---

[1]Maxwell Maltz, M.D., *Psycho-Cybernetics*, Pocket Books, Inc., New York, n.d.

*To love yourself is to accept
yourself, the good and the not-so-good*

The amazing thing is that many of these "heroes" go through life
saying exactly the same thing about others: "If only I was like
them, then I could really. . . . "

The sooner you face up to the fact that you will never be anyone
but yourself and start looking inside yourself for all the good
that's stored there, the sooner you will be on the *right road*
toward finding your niche—the success you deserve. You might
as well accept and love yourself because if you don't, just who do
you think is going to? Remember that while you're wasting your
time "if-ing," there are a lot of people out there making success
happen—earning good money, living in fine homes, and enjoying
themselves. They are the same as you, but they're not "if-ing";
they're making it happen!

What is really wrong with you? Possibly a lot of things, and
possibly very few. Don't dwell on negatives. No employer is going
to hire you because of them.

So why aren't you more successful?

There are a number of possibilities:
1. Perhaps you haven't established your goals.
2. Maybe you just haven't exploited your unique talents,
   interests, skills, and abilities.
3. Maybe you just don't know who you are.
4. Perhaps you just haven't known what you've wanted.

There's an even greater probability that you've been selling
yourself short, giving in to those inner fears of "I can't" when you
really can. You'll find that all you have to do is take the first
step—change one little thing, and the whole course of events in
your life may start to change. That one thing could quite possibly
be your attitude.

Everyone has problems. All the people who are more successful
than you have problems, but a lot of them owe their success to the
fact that they've learned how to deal with their problems and how
to overcome their shortcomings. Most of their secrets are set forth
in this book.

Remember that people who reach the top remain there as long
as they recognize that there is no such thing.

"But," you say, "I don't even know where or how to start." Let's begin at the beginning. "Beginning" is a very important word. Do you remember that saying, "Today is the first day of the rest of my life"? Start saying it now, and every day from now on, but add something to it: "And what am I going to do with it?" Don't say, "I wonder what's going to happen today?" Each new day is a new beginning for you—a never-look-back beginning.

Negative thoughts and looking back

Perhaps the Lord was trying to tell us something in the story of Sodom and Gomorrah, in which the people who looked back turned into pillars of salt. Perhaps if there were a penalty for looking back—for self-recrimination and negative thinking—we'd all be far ahead of where we are now. Well, there *is* such a penalty, and it is tremendous!

Every great journey begins with the first step. This important journey—your job hunt—must be a totally positive experience. It's concerned with the identification of the *unique you*. Work each of the exercises carefully. You'll be using all the discoveries you make and the insights you gain later on in your efforts.

Why not try an experiment? Each time you think a negative thought or are critical of yourself or someone else (critical people are usually the ones who don't like themselves), put a dollar or so into a special pocket earmarked for charity or wait another day to purchase something you really want and need. The sacrifice you make must hurt enough so that you'll be forced to think positively—and make this a habit. Here's another commandment: *Thou shalt recognize that positive thinking is your greatest asset and that negative thinking is your greatest enemy.*

A sounding board

These exercises must be worked by one person—you! You must depend upon yourself for their successful completion. However, a sounding board in the form of a fellow professional can be extremely helpful. This person (your mentor) should be someone with whom you have an honest and straightforward relationship and whose opinions you respect. Tell this person of your plans and ask for his or her support and assistance. Don't enlist the aid of a close friend or your spouse, who is too close and won't want to hurt your feelings when the time comes to be completely honest.

Arrange to meet with this person one evening each week to discuss and go over your progress, your exercises, and your growth in these efforts. Your mentor's responsibility will be to listen to you and ask questions such as:

1. Why have you chosen this as a goal?
2. Why do you feel this is an accomplishment?
3. Why do you feel this is a unique skill, talent, or ability?

This person must avoid becoming involved in his or her own concerns at this point. However, your mentor will gain a great deal from this experience. Acting as your critic and teacher will prove valuable and rewarding.

Steps in your career development

In this chapter, you'll be doing exercises concerned with the following steps in your career development:

Step 1. Establishing your goals

Step 2. Identifying your unique talents, interests, and abilities

Step 3. Pinpointing your skills

Step 4. Identifying your career choices

Step 5. Achieving self-acceptance and self-confidence

These exercises will help you to discover who you are and to lay the foundation for your ongoing career development.

"But," you say, "I already know who I am." Do you? You cannot sell a product effectively unless you truly know it and can specifically verbalize its assets and potential benefits. Similarly, it's important for you to know yourself and to develop a sales and marketing campaign for yourself. This will require a *written* effort on your part.

"Oh brother," you say, "something I've always been terrible at is writing." Most people feel that way. The fact that you've had problems in the past doesn't mean a thing. You are starting on a new life and a new program (a totally positive experience), and there's no time like the present to start learning—by doing.

This chapter—this book—is based on the philosophy that *people who have taken the time to discover who they really are have never been disappointed.* Why should you be afraid of finding out who you really are? I promise you, it is a worthwhile experience that will bring fantastic rewards, in the form of reinforcing your self-confidence and teaching you a lot about communicating.

As you do the exercises, it will be easy to think in terms of "can't" and "won't." For example, you've heard people say:

1. "I can't do it because I only have a high school diploma."
2. "It won't work because I'm too short."
3. "I can't do it because I'm a man."
4. "I can't do it because I'm a woman."

Don't statements like these sound ridiculous when someone else makes them? Believe me, they sound the same coming from you.

I've done all kinds of exercises recommended by various authors, and I've come to one conclusion: Those which I've outlined will bring the greatest results in the shortest period of time.

Another question

How will you know whether you're doing the exercises right? The only answer is that you'll know by the gut feeling you have while you're doing them and by the sense of satisfaction and self-confidence you will have when they're completed.

Again, these exercises have one purpose and one purpose only: to give you an appreciation of yourself and your unique abilities to contribute—a sense of self-confidence based on introspection and a belief in yourself.

The importance of writing it down

This chapter isn't going to work miracles. You and only you can make them happen. The answers aren't going to jump out at you from these pages. Remember that anything that's worthwhile takes effort. There are no shortcuts here and no easy way out. If that's what you want, please put this book in the trash or give it to someone who will appreciate it. And so another commandment: *Do it right—the first time.*

"OK," you say, "I know myself and my abilities, my likes and my dislikes. I don't have to do a lot of exercises to determine this." I said the same thing. After doing the exercises in my head, I convinced myself that even though they were pretty entertaining, they were so much wasted time and effort. I wanted to get on with it—to get that job. *I was wrong!* I really didn't know myself—my abilities, skills, interests, goals, and capabilities. I just thought I did until I wrote out the exercises in detail. Incidentally, if you don't believe me, just turn to Chapter 10 and try answering some of the stress questions. Then you'll see exactly what I mean.

A computer

Your brain has frequently been likened to a computer—a very compact, complex, and miraculous computer. Seemingly, it has unlimited potential just waiting to be tapped. But just like every other computer, it is totally useless unless it's properly programmed and produces the correct printout. So:

1. Sit down and relax.
2. Establish a reasonable (achievable) daily goal; i.e., program yourself.
3. Do research on the specific subject you plan to work on. Take lots of notes.
4. Make an outline (so that you will be able to see the forest in spite of the trees).
5. Start writing the answers down— produce your printout.

The job hunt

I want you to share my view that the job-hunting process can be an exciting adventure—like a safari in the jungle of the business world. However, if you do all the exercises in a haphazard manner and then find that you have to do them all over again, it will be like going hunting and finally spotting your game, only to discover that you've left your ammunition at home. If you have to go back home, get your ammunition, and start the hunt again, the original excitement will be lost.

Enlist your subconscious

The following exercises can't be done one at a time and then forgotten. Insight and recall don't work that way. As you begin to do the exercises, assign each problem to your subconscious—your computer. You will discover that as you do one exercise, ideas regarding the others will come to you. These thoughts must be recorded and not lost. Keep all the exercise sheets on your desk. As each new idea presents itself, record it and then get back to the exercise you're working on.

You might well find that your best thoughts occur to you while you are in the shower, shaving, or on the way to work. Keep a pencil and a small notebook handy—or, even better, pocket tape recorder. Record your thoughts—they'll prove valuable.

Step 1. *Establishing your goals*

The following excerpts from *The Fine Art of Doing Better*[2] (a book written by a number of America's finest motivational experts) and Zig Ziglar's book entitled *See You at the Top*[3] should stimulate you to set goals for yourself and give you an insight into the importance of goals in all your activities:

> Goals are important because it is as difficult to reach a destination you do not have, as it is to come back from a place you have never been.[4]
>
> Give me a stock clerk with a goal, and I will give you a man who will make history. Give me a man without a goal and I will give you a stock clerk.[5]
>
> Goals must be specific, clearly defined and well laid out.[6]
>
> Go as far as you can see and when you get there, you will be able to see further.[7]

Goals are rungs on the ladder to success (once you've climbed them, they are achievements). The two main members of the ladder are persistence and determination. The higher you climb this ladder, the finer the view and the greater the challenges and opportunities (unless you have a fear of heights).

Why don't most people want to establish goals? Probably because they don't know how to establish them, or possibly they don't know what goals are and why they're important. But the most basic reasons are fear of failure and procrastination.

Businesses and governments talk of achieving goals, and most of us have personal goals in the back of our minds. Somehow, however, our personal goals are always at the planning end of "if" rather than at the right end—the receiving end, the persistence and action end.

Let's look at goals more closely. Most of us, on a day-to-day basis, are concerned with goals like these:

Getting up in the morning
Going to work

[2]John Hammond (ed.), *The Fine Art of Doing Better,* American Motivational Association, Los Angeles, 1974. Author's royalties donated to Junior Achievement Inc.
[3]Zig Ziglar, *See You at the Top*, Pelican, Gretna, Louisiana, 1974.
[4]Ibid., p. 105.
[5]J. C. Penny, quoted in Hammond, op. cit., p. 105.
[6]Ziglar, op. cit., p. 106.
[7]Ibid., p. 268.

Having lunch
Making it through the day

These are immediate goals; next come the short-term ones, such as:

Getting a car
Getting a raise or a promotion

Why not think in terms of intermediate- and long-term goals? Make your future meaningful; by setting goals, you're programming your success.

The problem with goals

Goals must be written down, just like these exercises, and they must be referred to on a continuing basis. You might wish to refer to Appendix C for a daily assistance device. Remember that unwritten or unspoken goals are much too easy to forget.

How to establish goals

Open your mind—relax. No negative thinking is allowed. Ask yourself, "If I could have anything I wanted—be anything or do anything—what would it be?"

Now make a list of your goals. Progress one step at a time. Remember, "The elevator to success is out of order—you'll have to use the stairs—one step at a time."[8] Your goals must be:

1. Realistic and attainable.
2. Established in step fashion, with each related to the other. Start with long-term goals and then work backward to intermediate-term and short-term ones.
3. Set within a time frame for achievement.

The term "goal" somehow has acquired the connotations of "unattainable," "lofty," and "long-term." This is mostly wrong. If you methodically set your goals one step at a time and establish a time frame for achieving them, your far-off goals won't have to remain just that—far off! Let's look at some examples.

Long-term goals: These are your destinations—for example, the position of vice president, national marketing manager, or chief engineer. Your time frame could be five to ten years.

Intermediate-term goals: These are the milestones on your highway to success—a substantial raise with a promotion, for example. Your time frame might be two to five years.

[8]Hammond, op. cit., p. 268.

Short-term goals: These might be the steps you foresee as necessary for achieving your intermediate- and long-term goals. You might think of them as your step-by-step efforts. An example would be finding a good solution to a current problem your company is facing. Your time frame could be a year or less.

Remember that your goals can be both position- and possession-oriented. Keep them in mind constantly. Make them happen!

"Well," you say, "one thing is for sure. To accomplish all these goals, I'll have to make sure I'm in the right position and in the right industry. Also, with many positions as well as whole industries suddenly becoming outdated, it's important for me to be continually prepared for a career change."

Step 2. Identifying your unique talents, interests, and abilities

In this whole universe, there is only one *unique you*! This uniqueness, combined with your knowledge, experience, and skills, is very important and should be pointing you in a definite direction—toward happiness and self-fulfillment. However, unless you use your talents—yes, exploit them—there's a good possibility that you won't find the happiness and fulfillment you are searching for in life. Your talents and abilities are constantly seeking expression. Identify them, study them, develop them, and use them to become the successful person you know you can be.

Begin by speaking with your friends and members of your family. Ask them about your accomplishments in life and about any *unique* traits and abilities they've noticed. Ask as many questions as possible to bring out the "what" and "why" in their appraisal of you. *Write their comments down, no matter how insignificant they may seem.* Then, find a quiet place and go over them. Do a brainstorming session with yourself. This is "let-yourself-go" time. Look for a pattern. Are these appraisals of you pointing in some specific direction?

You could also make a listing like the following:

My parents always felt that I should be a _____ because
_____ .

I never somehow could see myself in that position because
_____ but perhaps they might have noticed certain unique facets of my personality which might better be used in _____ .

My peers in the office have been remarking about my abilities in the _____ area. Perhaps by exploring this area, I can add a new dimension to my current position or seek a new career field—a different position which will enable me to express this unique talent.

I've always wanted to _____ , but somehow I've never taken the bull by the horns and done it. The reasons I've wanted to _____ are: . . .

Now you have the idea. Come up with some additional talents and abilities which you can exploit. Write these down and explore them.

If you're having trouble understanding the "why" of this exercise, you might read Chapters 3 to 5 of *How to Make a Habit of Success*, by Bernard Haldane.[9] This book will explain the subject completely and give you some in-depth insights. Still another book—*Sun Signs*, by Linda Goodman[10]—will provide valuable insights and add some fun to this effort.

Now take all your research efforts and combine them. Do your unique accomplishments and talents point to a different vocation or perhaps to stressing different functions of your present position? Look for a pattern.

Step 3. Pinpointing your skills

"Skills." That word can scare a lot of people, but what they fear is simply the unknown. Because *Parachute*[11] does such an excellent job with this problem, I'm going to present some quotations and diagrams from it. First, though, look at Figure 1, which is a simple, straightforward, and understandable breakdown of skills from the introduction to volume II of the *Dictionary of Occupational Titles*,[12] as modified by Richard N. Bolles.[13] You'll note that the lesser skills are at the bottom, and the higher ones at the top.

[9]Bernard Haldane, *How to Make a Habit of Success*, Acropolis Books, Washington, 1975, revised edition, 1960 original edition.

[10]Linda Goodman, *Sun Signs*, Taplinger Publishing Co., Inc., New York, 1968.

[11]Richard N. Bolles, *What Color Is Your Parachute? A Practical Manual for Job-Hunters and Career-Changers*, rev. ed., Ten Speed Press, Berkeley, Calif., 1977.

[12]U.S. Department of Labor, Employment and Training Administration, *Dictionary of Occupational Titles*, 3d ed., Washington, 1965.

[13]Bolles, op. cit., p. 77. Used by permission of the author.

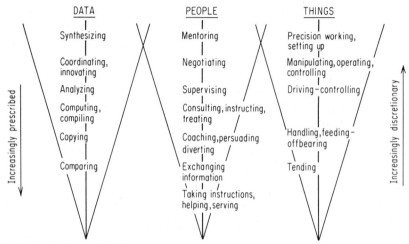

Fig. 1. Breakdown of skills

If you graded all these skills in terms of how many of their duties are prescribed in detail vs. how many are discretionary, i.e., left to the discretion of the employee, you would discover that the lower the skill, the more its duties are prescribed, with comparatively little discretion left to the employee; but, the higher the skill, the less its duties are prescribed, and the more that is left to the discretion of the employee.

Note, as we progress to higher levels of skills, how it becomes harder and harder for a prospective employer (say) to draw up a job description for this skill.

Each higher skill level usually or typically involves all those which preceded it.[14]

Incidentally, you'll want to note the definitions of each of these skills in the *Dictionary of Occupational Titles*[15] and relate them to your own.

The point of all this for you, the career changer/job-hunter, is:
1. The lower the level of your skills that you claim, the more the skills can be prescribed and measured and demanded of you. You'll have to fit in. Conversely, the higher the level of skills that you can legitimately claim, the less the skills can be prescribed and measured, and the more you will be free to carve out a job in the shape of you—making the fullest use of the special constellation of abilities that are you.

[14]Ibid., p. 78. Used by permission of the author.
[15]U.S. Department of Labor, op. cit., vol. II, pp. 649–650.

2. The higher level of skills that you can legitimately claim, either with people, or data or things (or, in varying degree, with all three) depending on what you want to do—the less these kinds of jobs are advertised or known through normal channels; the more you'll have to find ways of unearthing them.

3. Just because the opportunities for the higher level jobs (or careers) are harder to uncover, the higher you aim, the less people you will have to compete with—for that job. In fact, if you uncover, as you are very likely to, a need in the organization (or organizations) that you like, which you can help resolve, they are very likely to create a brand new job—for you, which means—in effect—you will be competing with practically no one, since you are virtually the sole applicant, as it were.[16]

Once you've pinpointed your skills, your goals will be to use and develop them effectively in conjunction with your gifts, interests, talents, and abilities. Now you're starting to see that it's not your lack of attributes that's been standing in your way. It's been your failure to recognize and use them effectively and to combine them with definitive goals that's been the roadblock.

Step 4. Identifying your career choices

Now that you've identified your goals, interests, talents, abilities, and skills, you can speak knowingly and specifically about what you are able to contribute. You have partially armed yourself— prequalified yourself so that you'll be able to conduct yourself professionally at those upcoming interviews.

The fact that you may have made a few mistakes in your career or chose the wrong major at college doesn't mean that you have to suffer for this the rest of your life or consider yourself a loser. If you are not sure that you've chosen the right career or if you don't have one or more alternative career choices that you're considering, the following exercise is important. Even if you're sure you're in the right job, this exercise will serve to reaffirm your present position and career choice and will give you additional insights and food for thought.

This exercise requires two steps. First, go to the library and, in

[16]Bolles, op. cit., pp. 78–79. Used by permission of the author.

the reference section, find the *Dictionary of Occupational Titles.*[17] Then get *Making Vocational Choices: A Theory of Careers,* by John L. Holland.[18] These books will give you the immediate, hard-hitting answers you're looking for. The first chapter of Holland's book will give you a good idea of what the rest of the book is about. Then turn to the appendixes. Read them and work each of the exercises. You'll be amazed at how many career areas you are qualified for and can contribute to. The exercises Holland suggests will give you ammunition for your hunt. Whether you have decided on one career area or a combination of several, these exercises will help you immensely in taking the first steps in the right direction.

As with the "skills step," the results you achieve will be directly related to the *Dictionary of Occupational Titles,*[19] which contains a wealth of information relating directly to your efforts. It consists of two volumes and a supplement.

Pay close attention to pages XV to XXIV in the introduction to volume I of the *Dictionary.* Here you will learn how to match your skills and vocational interests with available jobs. The *Dictionary* provides a method of identifying vocations and of pinpointing the specific skills needed for each one. Each occupation has a code number composed of six digits. The first three indicate the occupational group, and the second three indicate the level of skills required. This system might sound involved, but it's really quite simple.

Volume I also lists types and definitions of jobs (21,741 of them, alphabetically arranged). The definitions answer the questions of "what," "why," and "how." They also include miscellaneous information such as functions performed; aptitude, interests, and temperament required; and extraordinary physical demands involved.

Volume II of the *Dictionary* lists additional fields for your consideration (pages 3 to 24) and worker-trait groups (pages 217 to 529). Skills are discussed in detail on pages 649 to 650.

That's the end of this group of exercises, which are the most effective ones, in my estimation. Like you, I hate exercises; I don't want to waste my valuable time. But believe me, you can do these in a relatively short period of time and get the results you want. I ask one thing of you: Be honest with yourself. If you have

---

[17]U.S. Department of Labor, op. cit.

[18]John L. Holland, *Making Vocational Choices: A Theory of Careers,* Prentice-Hall, Inc., Englewood Cliffs, N.J., 1973.

[19]U.S. Department of Labor, op. cit.

done the exercises and still haven't acquired an understanding of, and an appreciation for, yourself, go back and do more exercises, supplementing the ones I've recommended with some from *Parachute.*[20] Remember that you can't expect an employer to appreciate you if you don't appreciate yourself.

Step 5. Achieving self-acceptance and self-confidence

Now that you've done these exercises, how will you put them to use? All this time and effort must not go to waste. First, you will be using them to present yourself in a new and unique manner, which will be explained in later chapters. Additionally, you will want to continually add to these and update them throughout your entire career; this is an important facet of your ongoing career development. Remember that self-marketing is a continuing responsibility, not something you do only when you're seeking a new position.

Be objective about yourself; remember the basics and keep everything in its proper perspective. Your ego, your emotions, and many other factors can keep you from achieving your goals or even from remembering them. When the going gets rough, your emotions are just waiting to come into play. This is when you need some support.

Your success manual: blueprint for success

I suggest that you make up your own success manual—as a wall to lean against. This should be a loose-leaf portfolio, something that you can refer to and use constantly. It should be your ongoing career development source, enabling you to evaluate your own professional progress and growth. You should put your manual in loose-leaf form because you're going to want to add to it and keep track of your progress and growth. Don't leave out anything; you will want to be able to look both backward and forward to see how you've progressed in your program and how your thinking has changed. This is ego-reinforcing.

Initially, you should use this blueprint to structure your career as you've projected it; then use it to keep in mind the goals you have established. For example, say that several months after accepting a position, you find you've run into tremendous

---

[20]Bolles, op. cit.

difficulties—a power play. Suddenly you are in a situation in which you're so involved that you can't see the forest for the trees. Your authority is being usurped, your responsibilities are being taken away, and so forth. You are starting to lose your self-confidence and direction. In addition to using the Success Minder referred to earlier in the goals exercise (Appendix C), you should refer to your manual. It will enable you to review:

1. Your goals—short-, intermediate-, and long-term
2. What you must do to accomplish these goals
3. Your unique skills, talents, and abilities, as a way to reinforce your self-confidence
4. Other matters which will be covered in later chapters

In short, then, your personal blueprint for success will provide you with a quick inventory of all that will reinforce your attitude and your self-image.

At this point, you'll be able to determine whether you're at a temporary roadblock, a detour, or merely a bump in relation to your career and professional development. Remember that career development is a continuing process (just like marketing) and that your wants and needs are continually changing. This portfolio will help you change and grow, while keeping your ultimate objective in mind.

Companies change, business conditions and attitudes change. While companies might want and need certain attributes in a person today, their expectations may well change as time goes on. Accordingly, you must constantly refresh and update yourself and your portfolio to reflect these changes and to develop yourself within the company and industry of your choosing. If you don't follow this program in an organized manner, you will face the problem of boredom as a result of needless repetition. Every time a position change, a career change, a promotion, etc., occurs, repeating your efforts becomes a formidable task.

By developing this portfolio, you will be methodically accomplishing simple goals; you will be breaking the overall problem down into its separate parts, solving each of these individual parts, and finally reaching your goal. Your manual for success will also allow you to continually identify and add performable functions; then, if a career or position change becomes necessary, you have a ready reference source.

Your manual should be broken down into the following sections.

Section 1: The first section should be composed of your goals. You should put these in the front so that you can refer to them quickly in order to remind yourself of where you are and where you plan to be.

Section 2: The next section in your manual should be your plan of action. This is your marketing program. You will want to refer to it on a continuing basis to see how you're coming along with your plan and program.

Section 3: This section should consist of the exercises presented in this chapter, except the ones concerned with goals.

Section 4: In this section you should include all the companies which are of interest to you and in which you feel qualified to hold a position. Include also the names of people in these companies who can be of help to you.

Section 5: This section consists of consulting interview information. It should include your work sheets, consulting interview evaluation sheets for each company contacted, and consulting questionnaire sheets, with answers from each person you have contacted. Also include thank-you letters and other pertinent correspondence.

Section 6: This section should contain interview preparation materials:

1. A review of information about the three to five industries you have chosen and the companies within those industries
2. Exercises involving questions and stress questions at an interview
3. Notes from your interview preparation

Section 7: This section consists of information developed from Chapters 9 and 12:

1. Your personal profile
2. Your performance description
3. Various job descriptions
4. Copies of any application forms you have completed

A matter of style

A certain amount of criticism might be leveled at this chapter and the following one because they require so much outside reading. Some people like doing a lot of reading, and others don't. They want to acquire information in a different way. One way isn't necessarily better than the other—it's just a matter of style.

I am not talking about cramming for an exam here; I am talking about your career—your future—and about how to select the right position for yourself in the right industry, the right company, and the right department. My only motive is to help you grow and succeed, something that you can achieve only by doing a lot of research. Be flexible. Do what is most comfortable for you, but don't cheat yourself—don't compromise your future.

One final note

Exposure's the name of the game. In the next chapter we'll attack the problem from another angle. You will learn to arm yourself for the hunt in a way that will guarantee—as far as possible—your choosing the right industry, company, and position.

FOUR

Your Potential Employers: All about Them

Knowing as much as possible about your potential employers is very important. It helps you to understand them and empathize with them. And, most certainly, it loads the odds for success in your favor.

In the previous chapter, we worked on identifying *you*. Here we'll work on target marketing—how to target your efforts so that they'll make the right position happen. In Chapter 3 you did a number of exercises. Maybe you also supplemented these with additional ones from *Parachute.*[1] Now is the time to start using the fruits of your labors.

Targeting your efforts

One exceptionally successful segment of the marketing fraternity is placing tremendous emphasis on target marketing. In essence, this approach is concerned with the same marketing effort explained in the Preface, but with the emphasis on the

[1]Richard N. Bolles, *What Color Is Your Parachute? A Practical Manual for Job-Hunters and Career-Changers*, rev. ed., Ten Speed Press, Berkeley, Calif., 1977.

satisfaction of customer needs within a very specifically identified (targeted) market segment.

Like these successful marketers, you will want to carve your niche by targeting (focusing) your efforts—by eliminating all the industries which hold no interest for you (or vice versa). You will want to concentrate your efforts on those three to five industries or career clusters which are truly worthy of your consideration.

This is a chore, but it can be made relatively simple. There are at least 88 million employment opportunities out there. Of those 88 million, possibly some could be eliminated (i.e., people who just aren't doing the job), but probably a lot more could be *created*. This latter area is, of course, where you'll want to concentrate your efforts. Why? Well, in addition to all the obvious reasons, experts tell us that 50 percent or more of all positions which are filled are newly created.

How do you go about cutting these jobs and career opportunities down to a manageable number? Furthermore, how do you go about determining which positions you'd be best suited to fill?

Cutting it down

Your immediate goal is to identify the fifteen to twenty-five companies where you can make a contribution—where you can be happy and "do your thing." A good rule of thumb might be to pick five industries directly related to the vocations you selected in the vocational identification exercise in the previous chapter. Then choose three to five companies in each industry where you can target your efforts properly and effectively.

I really don't believe anyone knows how many occupational clusters or career opportunities there are in this country. Some experts feel that 35,000 is a good number; others say there are a lot more. The actual figure is not really important. Your concern is to work with something which is manageable. Let's use the government's listing of sixteen broad vocational groupings:

1. Construction
2. Manufacturing
3. Transportation
4. Consumer affairs and homemaking
5. Personal services
6. Fine arts and humanities
7. Hospitality and recreation
8. Health

9. Environmental control
10. Public services
11. Marine sciences
12. Agribusiness and natural resources
13. Marketing and distributive
14. Business and office
15. Communications and media
16. New and emerging

Now, match and compare your vocational choices from Chapter 3 with these sixteen occupational groupings. Choose the five which are of the greatest interest to you and note how closely they are related. Definitions of each of the above occupational clusters and specific occupational information breakdowns can be found in both the *Dictionary of Occupational Titles*[2] and the *Occupational Outlook Handbook.*[3] We shall get into these shortly.

Making knowledgeable and informed choices

Finding out about potential employers will require a reasonable amount of research and introspection on your part. Where do you start? One of the most frustrating problems you'll face will be that no one seems to know where to find career information. I'm going to go into considerable detail on the subject of career information to help you save time and avoid frustration.

First, make up a file folder for each of the five industries of greatest interest to you. Include a separate file here for industry information. Next make up twenty-five file folders for the companies in those industries which you'll identify and work with. Remember that the knowledge and self-awareness you will acquire as a result of doing this yourself and doing it right will make you that much stronger and more confident.

Industry information sources

Let's begin by identifying industry information sources. Perhaps the most valuable sources for this kind of information are found in the financial community. It is the responsibility of members of the financial community to be fully abreast of the "action"—

[2]U.S. Department of Labor, Employment and Training Administration, *Dictionary of Occupational Titles*, 3d ed., Washington, 1965.
[3]U.S. Department of Labor, Bureau of Labor Statistics, *Occupational Outlook Handbook*, 1976–1977 ed., Washington.

financial and otherwise—so that they can be of service to their clients.

Large, "full-service" stockbrokerage firms

Many of the small firms don't have research departments that can provide you with large, in-depth industry research reports. Furthermore, they usually insist that you have an account with them before they will even speak with you about their research information. Large firms provide excellent industry information brochures for review of investment opportunities within specifically identified industries. These reports go into considerable detail regarding past histories, present and anticipated developments, and (perhaps most important) reasons for anticipated growth or stability in the future. What could give you more ammunition for your efforts?

These same brokerage firms will usually subscribe to *The Value Line Investment Survey*.[4] This continually updated industry and company information source contains excellent analyses of industry groupings and ratings of industries and companies within those industries.

While you're there, be sure to note the Standard and Poor's[5] information sheets on specifically listed publicly owned corporations—listed on the major exchanges or traded over the counter. Each of these sheets will provide you with detailed, pertinent information about the companies of your choice.

Research departments of large banks and savings and loan organizations

These financial institutions have a considerable responsibility to their portfolio and investment departments to keep them informed regarding industry prospects and developments. These responsibilities include knowing which industries and companies are growing as well as which ones are declining. The relevant departments must be apprised of all current and anticipated developments. You will be amazed at how much information these research departments can give you regarding local and regional industry growth and developments.

Remember, however, that financial institutions are not in business to assist people in making career choices. They exist to sell stocks, bonds, and commodities and to promote their finan-

---

[4]*The Value Line Investment Survey*, Arnold Bernhard & Co., Inc., New York.
[5]*Standard N.Y.S.E. Stock Reports*, Standard and Poor's Corporation, New York.

cial services. Employees of these firms are responsible to their employers and to their clients. When you ask them for research materials and information, you are asking a favor. Wait until *after* market hours.

The reference section of your library

Another source of information about a specific industry is the reference section of your local library. Ask for information regarding industries and career opportunities. You might well be directed to one of the better sources for the career information you're seeking: the *Encyclopaedia of Careers and Vocational Guidance.*[6]

This two-volume encyclopaedia was designed to help students, teachers, career changers, and those concerned with career development.

Volume I includes five articles written by authorities in vocational guidance. I recommend that you read them. They will give you information to supplement your efforts in Chapter 3 concerning identification of your interests, aptitudes, and skills. Volume I also contains over seventy articles on opportunities in major industries written by top people in their fields.

Volume II gives additional information on career opportunities; there are 220 articles on occupations which might be of interest to you. Check these over carefully.

Government publications

The U.S. Department of Labor, Bureau of Labor Statistics, publishes an excellent handbook (truly more of a large directory), to which I have already referred. This is the *Occupational Outlook Handbook.* Published annually, it contains a wealth of information. You can obtain a copy for $7 by writing to Superintendent of Documents, Government Printing Office, Washington, D.C. 20402. The *Handbook* is probably available at your library, but there is a good chance that after seeing it, you'll want a copy for yourself.

The *Handbook* includes 300 occupational briefs, grouped into clusters of related positions, and thirty-five industry briefs. The *Handbook* also presents a lot of other valuable information. For example, it includes a rundown on 300 positions. For each position it outlines the following:

1. The nature of the work to be performed

---

[6]*Encyclopaedia of Careers and Vocational Guidance*, Doubleday, New York, 1975.

2. The places of employment
3. Training and qualifications required as well as an outline of opportunities for advancement
4. The employment outlook
5. Earnings and working conditions
6. Sources of additional information

As is true of any source material, you must remember that the authors of *The Encyclopaedia of Careers and Vocational Guidance* and the *Occupational Outlook Handbook* are presenting their opinions, and these might differ considerably from yours and/or those of people currently in the positions themselves. You must gather as much information as possible regarding each identified vocation and then make your own decisions. We shall say more about this later.

Once you have consulted these books, do the following exercise:

1. Open the *Handbook* and/or the *Encyclopaedia*[7] to the table of contents.
2. Read the entire list of occupations.
3. Make a note of every occupation in which you have the slightest interest (don't concern yourself with qualifications at this point).
4. *Keep an open mind.*
5. Go over your listing to see whether there is a pattern. Does it point to any new or different areas that you haven't included in your findings from the vocations exercise in Chapter 3?

Kiplinger Letters

Another excellent source for industry information is the Kiplinger Washington Letters (or demographically targeted Kiplinger Letters). These can give you good insights into the potential and growth of new industries and products.

Industry associations

Industry associations are also excellent sources of information. Each industry has one or several associations directly related to its activities. Additionally, there are many associations somewhat related to certain industry groupings. People who are association-oriented will be more than happy to help you in your

[7]Many of the people I've worked with consider these two reference sources to be the best available. Together they seem to bring everything into the proper perspective.

career efforts and to provide you with information and answers. But you do have to get out there and ask questions; the information won't come looking for you.

Industry-related publications

Industry-related publications—magazines, journals, newspapers, convention information, trade directories, and so on—can give you an excellent overview of happenings within an industry and closely related industries.

Private sources

There are also many private sources of industry information, but these are very expensive, and we won't go into them here. Remember that your major concern is to identify five industries in which to concentrate your efforts; then it will be easy to identify companies within those industries, as you will see.

Company information sources

Let's start by identifying outside sources of company information. Then we'll move to company-disseminated information and finally to government-supplied, company-disseminated information. Obviously, the sources mentioned above (financial institutions, industry associations, handbooks, and libraries) can also provide you with excellent individual company information, but the following sources are much more specific:

1. *The Wall Street Journal.* Available at newsstands, in libraries, etc. This is a daily publication, read by people who really want to be informed about industry, companies, and people—nationally and internationally.
2. *Barron's.* Available at newsstands, in libraries, etc. This weekly publication provides a wealth of insights.
3. *Dunn's Review.*
4. *Business Week.*
5. *Forbes.*
6. *Fortune.*[8]
7. The business and finance section of your local newspapers.

Now that your files are set up, you must stay informed, not only about your own company and its products and services, but also about your company's competitors and about the industries

[8]Don't forget all the back issues of these publications at the library.

you've selected for your ongoing review. Cut interesting articles out of the newspaper. Make up your library of magazines or, better yet, keep copies of pertinent articles in your files. This will be a valuable source for all your ongoing career information and development efforts.

Outside sources of company information

The following information sources can usually be found at stockbrokerage firms:

1. Standard and Poor's corporation records
2. Dunn and Bradstreet reference library

The reference section of your local library will probably have copies of these sources:

1. *Thomas' Register of American Manufacturers*
2. Moody's manuals
3. State corporate directories, journals, and registers

These information sources usually list companies in a number of different ways for ease of identification. For example, a single company may have:

1. An alphabetical listing
2. A geographical listing (usually by city)
3. A product or services listing
4. An export and/or import listing

Here is what you can expect to find in such a reference source regarding a specific company:

Company name (and name of parent company if it is a subsidiary)
Company mailing address (if post office box)
Company address (street address)
City, state, and zip code
Phone number (including area code)
SIC number (standard industrial code)
Date established (in some cases)
Company officers and titles
Products manufactured or services rendered
Number of employees
Sales rating or specific sales figures

These listings might include additional information, such as number of divisions and location of the home office, branch plants, sales offices, and affiliates. SIC is explained in detail in the introductory section of each of the reference sources.

Detailed company-disseminated information

Annual reports: Company annual reports provide perhaps the most complete information generally available. You can usually obtain a company report either by asking in person or mailing in a request.

Reports of government regulatory agencies: If you feel you want extremely detailed information, you might request a copy of the company's 10K filing from the Securities and Exchange Commission. (This, of course, will be available for companies which are publicly owned.) Publicly traded companies will also file other in-depth information—8K reports, 10Q reports (filed on a quarterly basis), proxy statements, and more. In large population centers, this information will be available on microfiche. You will have to go personally to one of the SEC offices and ask for this, but the excellent in-depth information you obtain will prove to be well worth your while. (Don't overlook companies that are privately owned; there are some very large ones.)

Detailed information regarding all companies, public and private, can be found in the regular reports of such governmental agencies as:

1. The Federal Communications Commission
2. The Federal Power Commission
3. The Interstate Commerce Commission
4. The Federal Trade Commission
5. The Federal Reserve Board

Don't overlook information from state regulatory agencies.

How do you get your hands on this material? Libraries in major cities will have government depository sections. Ask to speak with the government documents librarian; this person can be an excellent source of information. You can also write to the regulatory agency responsible for companies within your identified area of interest. Under the Freedom of Information Act, you can request copies of a specific company's annual reports to the regulatory agency (there will be a charge for duplication expenses, of course).

Other company disseminated information: Catalogs, brochures, sales literature, advertising samples, and company propaganda will give you information on specific company products and services. These sources should all prove helpful and informative.

Chosen geographic areas

Information about companies in specific geographic areas can readily be acquired from most of the above sources as well as the following:

1. Chambers of commerce. Many of these organizations publish directories which you may find helpful. Such a directory might give a company an alphabetical listing and a product or services listing and also provide miscellaneous information on realtors and restaurants, for example.
2. National moving companies. These frequently provide excellent information as one of their services.
3. The U.S. Department of Commerce. This department publishes a *Census of Selected Service Industries*, which contains a tremendous number of statistics and much valuable information on companies in individual state groupings.
4. The Yellow Pages of the phone book.

Caution: Remember that you should be concerned with opportunity, not company location. Location should be one of your smallest considerations. Don't let company location influence your vocational choice. If you do, you probably will regret it—over and over again.

People information sources

The following reference books will provide you with excellent information about the people who are heading up some of the companies of interest to you:

1. *Who's Who in American Industry*
2. Volume 2 of Standard and Poor's *Register of Corporations, Directors and Executives.* The in-depth information in these publications will help you to better understand the decision makers and appreciate their accomplishments.

Your personality

Is there a common denominator which can tie your potential for success to your choice of a position? Is there a denominator that can cut through established barriers and misconceptions—matching your particular qualities and experience with success? Quite possibly there is! That common denominator is personality.

The compatibility exercise shown in Figure 2 is meant to assist you in grouping yourself within a specific type or class of personality. To do this exercise, circle the number which best typifies or describes you. You'll note that the list is composed of opposites or antonyms. If you feel strongly that you have a certain personality characteristic, circle the number closest to that characteristic. For example:

Demands freedom 1___2___3___4___5___ Likes strong control

Here, if you felt strongly that you were a self-starter and that you didn't like to control people or be controlled, you would circle the number 1. On the other hand, if you had no strong feelings either way, you would place a mark in the center, between numbers 3 and 4.

Note that there are no right or wrong answers in this exercise. It is concerned only with self-acceptance and self-recognition. If you feel that you are not objective enough, have the mentor who's been working with you do the exercise with you.

An exercise—not a test

I'm sure that psychometrists across the country would throw up their hands in total dismay because of the "crudities" of this exercise. However, it is not meant to prove anything, and I make no claims for its validity. It is meant simply to draw your attention to the importance of personality matching—something which only you can do.

Before going any further, remember that decision makers, companies, and even industries have "personalities" all their own. Thus another important consideration is that of matching your personality to the personalities of the specific companies and industries on which you've decided to concentrate your efforts.

The corporate personality

Finding the right position requires that you identify corporate personality. There are probably as many corporate personalities as there are companies, but for the sake of simplicity let's categorize companies into five types:

	1	2	3	4	5	
Demands freedom	/	/	/	/	/	Likes strong control
Impatient	1	2	3	4	5	Patient
Risk oriented	1	2	3	4	5	Avoids risk
Unconcerned	1	2	3	4	5	Highly cautious
Off-the-cuff	1	2	3	4	5	Pensive
Ambitious	1	2	3	4	5	Staid
Showman	1	2	3	4	5	Reserved
Hard driving	1	2	3	4	5	Balanced
Apolitical	1	2	3	4	5	Highly political
Insecure	1	2	3	4	5	Secure
Haphazard	1	2	3	4	5	Detail oriented
Tenuous financially	1	2	3	4	5	Financially secure
Poor controls	1	2	3	4	5	Strict controls
Broad opportunity	1	2	3	4	5	Limited opportunity
Dislikes routine procedure	1	2	3	4	5	Memo strangled
No busywork	1	2	3	4	5	Thrives on busywork
Creative	1	2	3	4	5	Maintains status quo
Energetic	1	2	3	4	5	Ho-hum, mañana
Individual goal oriented	1	2	3	4	5	Company goal oriented
Poorly organized	1	2	3	4	5	Overly organized
Obsessive-compulsive	1	2	3	4	5	Unconcerned
Innovative	1	2	3	4	5	Let-it-be attitude
Swinger	1	2	3	4	5	Gray flannel suit
Confident	1	2	3	4	5	Dependent
Decisive	1	2	3	4	5	Avoids decisions
Disorganized	1	2	3	4	5	Highly organized
Loner	1	2	3	4	5	Groupie
Dislikes structure	1	2	3	4	5	Highly structured
Subtotals	___	___	___	___	___	

	1	2	3	4	5	
Decision oriented	/	/	/	/	/	Consensus seeking
Growth oriented	1	2	3	4	5	Status quo insistent
Doers	1	2	3	4	5	Talkers
Get it done	1	2	3	4	5	Maybe next week
Colorful	1	2	3	4	5	Plain
Irresponsible	1	2	3	4	5	Highly concerned
Unstable	1	2	3	4	5	Stable
Unpredictable	1	2	3	4	5	Highly predictable
Questionable mores	1	2	3	4	5	Semblance of ethics
Rejects authority	1	2	3	4	5	Accepts authority
Self-motivated	1	2	3	4	5	Unmotivated
Reasonable ethics	1	2	3	4	5	Lip service to ethics
Independent	1	2	3	4	5	Dependent
Giver	1	2	3	4	5	Taker
Charismatic	1	2	3	4	5	Blah
Fun demanding	1	2	3	4	5	Stoical
Liberal	1	2	3	4	5	Arch conservative
Let 'er rip	1	2	3	4	5	Corporate reserve
Down-to-earth	1	2	3	4	5	Plastic facade
Do it yourself	1	2	3	4	5	Whom else can we involve
Commitment to self	1	2	3	4	5	Commitment to system
Questioning	1	2	3	4	5	Blind loyalty
Aggressive thinker	1	2	3	4	5	Paid not to think
Individual	1	2	3	4	5	One of the masses
Controversial	1	2	3	4	5	Unquestioning
Dissenting	1	2	3	4	5	Yielding
Totals	___	___	___	___	___	

Fig. 2. Compatibility exercise

1. The high-roller operation
2. The entrepreneurial company
3. The autocratic company
4. The large corporation (big business)
5. The bureaucracy

I'm not going to define these terms for you. It's up to you to formulate your own personality types here. In fact, if you don't like these titles or if you feel that they aren't listed in the proper sequence, change them around until you feel comfortable with them. Of course, corporate personality types will vary considerably according to position and management level.

As in the previous exercise, there are no right or wrong types of operation. A high-roller operation isn't immoral or wrong, for example. Before you start this next page of the exercise, be sure you've completed the first part. The second part might tend to influence your answers on the first. You would only be hurting yourself.

In the compatibility exercise there are lines between the numbers. Return to that exercise and write the names of corporate personality types between the numbers. For example, between numbers 1 and 2, write "high-roller" (or another name); between numbers 2 and 3, write "entrepreneur" (or another name); and so on.

Now look for a pattern. Do you find that your personality characteristics cluster around a specific type of corporate personality? If that's the case, you should definitely seek an employer close to that personality type.

The differential can be considerable

Be aware that even though there may appear to be many similarities between adjacent personality types, each one is separate and distinct. A change from one type of company and industry to another can be difficult, even though the same personality type is required.

The differential between each type compounds itself as you move across the chart. A move from one type to an adjacent one can be good, but a move in the wrong direction or a move of two or more types could possibly be disastrous. The point is that once a business operation has forced you to mold your personality to fit the corporate personality, you may find it very difficult—even impossible—to reverse the process.

The further you move away from your identified personality type, the more intolerable your move will become, both for you and for your new employer, as you are about to see.

Some examples

If a bureaucracy employs a highly energetic, hard-hitting, verbal, flashy loner, both management and the employee are courting disaster. The employee's innovative ideas, along with his or her other unique characteristics, are directly opposed to the structured, political, status quo environment.

Now let's take the exact opposite situation. If a bureaucrat is employed by a high-roller company, both parties are also courting disaster. Management may have decided that some proved organizational skills combined with "all that knowledge" could be just what the company needs. Mr. Bureaucrat, in turn, is dissatisfied with his salary plus cost-of-living increases and with the day-in, day-out humdrum and is looking for some excitement. Here's his chance to make his mark with a go-go operation—to make it big and retire early.

In this example, there's a good possibility that both sides will get a lot more than they bargained for—mostly negatives, I'm sorry to add.

Let's look closely at the problem. If our bureaucrat had changed over to a large corporation or an autocracy, he might well have found the right position. But he didn't. So here are some of the things that happen:

Communication: He writes memos that management doesn't have the time to read. The other executives do a lot of fast talking, which he can't keep up with. They like to talk about sex and sports; he wants to talk about business.

Organization: He wants to hold a committee meeting to discuss a problem. The other executives would prefer to talk about it at a bar. If the effort proves to be successful, great! If it's unsuccessful, so much for that one. Either way, it's on to the next deal.

Tangibles versus intangibles: His major interest and knowledge are centered around tangible products for which there is a demand. The high-roller operation is concerned with concept sales, possibly stocks, commodities, insurance, leasing, raw land, and unique products that need to be promoted. That is, the company wants to create a demand.

Jack-of-all-trades versus master of one: He has been taught to relate within a very limited framework—a strong corporate structure, chain of command, etc. This is completely opposed to the manner in which Mr. Do-It-All thinks and works. He can't be bothered; there's too much money out there to be made, and there are too many deals to be put together.

You can see where this is leading. What I'm trying to say is that you should come as close as possible to matching your personality with that of your chosen employer-to-be. And keep in mind that there is no perfect example of a bureaucracy, a high-roller operation, or any of the other types. Often, however, you can categorize an organization on the basis of one outstanding characteristic, even though others are present. As you do research on each company's management, industry position, product, or service, you will find words used to describe the company's specific personality. They should enable you to do the necessary categorizing.

Companies change; people change

Just because a company is right for you today, this doesn't mean that it will be right for you in ten years or even five years. Companies and people change—thank God. Without change, there can be no progress. Some companies and people grow, some fail, and others mature and carry on. Don't fight the inevitable! Accept the fact that you will change and grow and that your attitudes and approaches to life will mellow. If you and your employer grow apart and you feel unhappy and unfulfilled, you must seriously consider finding an employer whose personality more closely matches your own. You will be doing a favor for yourself, your present employer, and your employer-to-be.

Let's look at an example of how such a change is sometimes dictated. Recognizing who you are and who your employer is might have two sides, which seemingly are at odds. On the one hand, you find that you possess most of the traits found at the high-roller end of the scale. On the other hand, you also recognize that in order to make it in the big time, you will need the best training possible. That training might be available only in the largest corporation dominating your industry. In this situation you might think it best to pocket your pride and your feelings (i.e., play the game) for two or three years, get the experience you need, and then move to a company which matches your personality and way of thinking more closely—a high-roller type of operation.

Come on now . . .

Am I saying that there's no room in bureaucracies for creative, innovative people? No, I'm not saying that at all. I'm saying that the price they must pay—ulcers, migraines, incredible frustration, and so on—is tremendous. Because of these people, bureaucracies *do* inch forward, seemingly in spite of all the bureaucrats. But these "doers" will continually be seeking to express their true personalities; they will be seeking to release and exploit their unrealized talents and abilities. They can be recognized by a devotion to stock market "dabbling," real estate speculation, backing new business ventures, gambling, and so on. I'm sure you have known people like this (perhaps there are some in your own office). If these people had recognized the importance of personality matching before they took their positions, they would probably be a lot happier, more successful, and more fulfilled today.

How to identify corporate personalities

You identify corporate personalities by doing research and asking questions. You will find that a great deal of classifying has already been done for you in the materials you've been reviewing. There are labels everywhere. Just look again.

Experience is marketable, but . . .

If you've been in the marketplace and are experienced, common sense dictates that you should seek out companies in your current field of endeavor as well as firms serving your industry. These companies will place the highest value on your services, your knowledge, and your experience.

Once you've checked into all these, you might do research on allied industries, e.g., those which make similar products or provide similar services. But, as discussed in Chapter 3, why not expand your horizons? There must be some reason for your current dissatisfaction. If you stay in the same industry, will you encounter the same problems you're currently striving to leave behind? As long as you're changing positions, you might even consider changing careers? Consider *all* the alternatives.

Remember that some people change careers as many as five times during their lives. But I hasten to add that changing careers is difficult. However, if a career change is in the cards—if you've made an error in your first, second, or even third career choice or if you've really picked a company with the wrong corporate personality—then you must recognize your mistake and do something about it. Life is all too short to spend it being miserable. You *can* get the right position. You *can* find your niche. Reading this book puts you way ahead, so dare to be successful.

Of course, the most valuable source for all this information is the decision makers themselves. We'll discuss how to meet these people in the next chapter.

A reminder

No matter what you do or how you do it, be sure you know as much as possible about the industry, the company and its personality, the people in the company, the competition, and the products of the industry before you even start thinking about interviewing. Your goal in these first four chapters has been to *prequalify* yourself for the right position.

Before you go any further, ask yourself the following questions: "Have I really exhausted all the available information sources regarding me and my potential employer?" "Am I fully prepared and informed?" Take your time. It's your life and your future.

FIVE

Exposure: The Finest Product— If Never Seen, Is Never Sold

All the effort you're expended so far will be meaningless unless you get results—results in the form of interviews, job offers, and the right position.

You've done a lot of research, but not the kind that will give you the answers to the questions you're really concerned with, questions such as:

1. What opportunities (if any) really exist?
2. How do I know whether I'll really like the company and the industry?
3. Will I be able to identify with the decision makers (and my future boss)?
4. Do I have anything in common with my potential coworkers? Will I like their ideas and philosophies?
5. Which position would I be best suited for?

But let's face it; first things first. How will you find the answers to these questions if you can't even get your foot in the door? If you come in as an applicant, chances are you'll get the "personnel shuffle," and that won't help you get those important answers.

Remember that the personnel department works from job requisitions, and experts tell us that perhaps 50 percent of a company's positions are newly created. You cannot get the position that you want to *create* through the personnel department because the people there don't even know that you and your unique potential to contribute exist. Personnel thinks that its job is to keep you from meeting the decision maker with comments like, "I'm sorry, there's nothing available at this time."

The decision makers: understanding them

Let's apply what we learned about the personnel function in Chapter 2. The decision maker and the personnel manager have the following in common when it comes to recruitment, review, interviewing, and selection responsibilities:

1. They get bored—in fact, frustrated.
2. They become negative and skeptical.
3. They dislike this part of their responsibilities.
4. They know that using an agency, newspaper ads, etc., can be very expensive and that there is little or no guarantee as to results.

Now that we know what the problems are, let's turn them into opportunities and solve them. Let's make this a pleasant experience both for you and for the decision maker. And it truly can be! But again, you must go one step at a time.

There's got to be a better way

There's got to be a better way than the usual ones of getting the answers you want and establishing the personal contact you need. How can both you and the decision maker get that important information *before* being put on the firing line in the formal interview situation?

In the usual initial or screening interview both you and the decision maker have difficulty being yourselves. How can you arrange to meet decision makers on an equal basis? How can you get them to talk to you "professional to professional"? How can you combine research and interviewing in a meaningful, productive manner?

One possible answer: the informal consulting interview

One possible solution to this problem might be to arrange for a personally conducted *informal consulting interview* with the decision maker. This is a friendly and relaxed get-together during which you accomplish the following:

1. You find out who the decision maker really is.
2. You get your foot in the door (gain exposure).
3. You bypass the personnel department and their interviews.
4. You seek the decision maker's professional advice and counsel regarding the industry and the company. In essence, you want to know about:
   a. The challenges of the industry
   b. The challenges of this company
   c. The challenges of this department (which could vitally concern you and your future)
5. You determine whether you can identify with this person, this company, and this industry.
6. You arrange for contacts and referrals for this effort and for all your future efforts.
7. You gain additional self-confidence.
8. You help yourself to get the right position a lot sooner than you would otherwise, and in a first-class manner.

During the consulting interview, you will be interviewing the decision maker. The onus will be on that person to inform and perhaps impress you and to provide advice and counsel. If you handle this properly, both you and the decision maker will be pleased with the results.

Remember that under no circumstances is this to be considered an interrogation or hearing. You are not grilling the decision maker or asking for a job. You are requesting a favor—to meet with this person—and since he or she has been kind enough to agree to this, you should be considerate and well prepared. Remember that a decision maker's time is valuable.

The consulting interview technique is an innovative, professional approach to executive job hunting. It depends for its success on a number of concepts that have been proved effective, the most important of which is *referral selling.*

You may look upon this technique as requiring a "bold-as-brass" approach—a thinly disguised "hard sell." You may consider yourself a "low-keyed professional," the "conventional operations type," the "traditional financial type," or the "introspective engineering type," for example. You ask yourself, "Can I effectively pull off this consulting interview?" A better question might be, "Can I, in my continuing career development efforts, afford *not* to pull it off?"

The consulting interview will be exactly what *YOU* make of it. It can be bold and aggressive or proper and professional. It all depends on you and your approach to life—your personality. Every facet of the consulting interview technique is carefully designed and planned to enable you to accomplish the purposes listed earlier in this chapter. Review that list now. Aren't all these things vitally important to your making informed decisions about your ongoing career development and about any position you might accept? No matter what your personality type, they *are* important.

You can do anything you truly want to do. It will require a certain degree of self-confidence, but you have a good start on that now. Successfully handling the consulting interview will reinforce your self-confidence; most other methods of job hunting don't do this. The commonsense appeal of this technique will also give you confidence. But let's get into it so that you can see for yourself.

How to arrange for the consulting interview

Although there are many techniques, overt and covert, for getting through the door, we're going to concentrate on the most straightforward and effective one: *referral.* How do you go about getting referred? You do this by using the telephone and all your contacts *knowledgeably.* We'll discuss the details below. The Career Search Work Sheet, shown in Figure 3, may be helpful to you as you set up contacts during your search.

How to manufacture referrals

The golden rule

Arranging interviews can be simple or difficult, and how well they turn out depends in large part on you and how you treat people. The receptionist or secretary can provide a wealth of assistance and information or can refer you to someone else who can. Good secretaries and receptionists must be "in the know." They're privy to information about who must (or will) be allowed to talk to whom. However, remember that they're usually busy, and so you must be courteous and warm and come straight to the point. For example:

"Hello, my name is _____, and I've been doing quite a bit of

CAREER SEARCH
WORK SHEET

Industry under consideration: _____ Start date: _____
Position(s) sought: _____

Company contacted, date (Starting with largest, to smallest)	Business phone number	Manager contacted Name_____Position_____Specialty			Response	Call when	Appointme when

Fig. 3

research in the _____ industry. Because your company is important in this field, I'd like some straight information. Could you please help me by referring me to the decision maker in the _____ department? Oh yes, and could you please spell his name for me? Thanks for your help; I really appreciate it."

or

"I need your help. Do you have a few seconds? I'm very interested in speaking with "the" person in the _____ department—you know, the one who makes the decisions. Could you possibly put me through? Oh yes, how do you spell her name? Thanks a lot."

or

"I'd like to direct some correspondence to the person who's responsible for the _____ department in your company. Could you tell me his name and title?"

This first, somewhat "bold" approach—referral through a secretary—should, however, really be used only as a last resort, and here's why. To make it work, you need an entrée like the following:

"Mrs. Jackie _____, vice president of marketing, suggested that I speak with you. She said that you are a very fine and helpful professional in this industry and could be of considerable assistance to me."

Unless you can say something like this, you're probably going to have to honestly answer the question, "How did you get my name?" Needless to say, being referred by a secretary or knowing an executive's name as a result of your outside research into business publications is not nearly as commanding or flattering as being referred by another executive.

"I need your help"

It's often the *way* you present yourself that makes the difference between failure and success, between class and brass. In studying the following examples, remember that your goal is to meet *personally* with the decision maker. To do this, you must make an appointment. When you introduce yourself to the decision maker, always say, "I need your help" (because it's true). Then go on to say something like, "I was hoping that you could spare a few minutes to give me the benefit of your knowledge and experience. Remember that "real people" need, like, and want to help. And so another commandment: *Thou shalt say, "I need your help."* When used honestly and effectively, this magic sentence can result in undreamed-of assistance and information. You will be amazed at how much information is available. All you need to do is ask. If you don't get the answers you want right away, just keep asking until you do.

Now let's look at some extremely effective methods of referral and introduction.

How to set up the interviews

Referral through a company manager or executive

You can invite an executive to breakfast or lunch, for example. This person could be someone you met at a local business convention, for example, or through a friend. (Even if he or she doesn't accept your invitation, it was still a nice gesture on your part.)

If you want to take a more aggressive approach, call and ask to speak with one of the people in the department you're interested in, or ask to speak to someone who's been with the company a while and can answer some questions in depth.

No matter which approach you use, tell the person that you need some help and would like to discuss the company, the industry, the product line, and so on. Ask whether you could possibly get together in a few days.

Referral through someone very knowledgeable about the company and the industry

This could be a competitor, perhaps, or a former employee. Contacts, as you well know, are extremely important—now and for the rest of your life. And so another commandment: *Thou shalt continually strive to make and maintain contacts.*

Once you have asked for and received someone's help in the form of a referral, it's your responsibility to assure this person that you won't violate confidences or jeopardize his or her relationship with the person to whom you are referred.

Referral through the "real people"

In every industry and company, you'll find at least a few "real people." These are the listeners—the ones who keep their ears to the ground and know what's happening and who needs whom, what, when, where, why, and how. Seek out these people by questioning your referral source, the secretary, or the receptionist or by asking for someone who might know who and where they are.

Referral through labor relations consultants

Ask a labor relations consultant who is knowledgeable about one of your chosen industries and well acquainted with the people and the problems of the industry for additional information and contacts. Labor relations consultants deal with the presidents and chief executive officers of companies. What better source could there be for your entrée?

Referral through a banker

Bankers have to know what's going on in the companies they lend money to.

Referral through corporate attorneys

These people can be excellent referral sources, but, again, identifying and getting through to them can be a real hassle.

Referral through manufacturers' representatives

Manufacturers' representatives have a major responsibility; they must know everything they can about what's happening and going to happen in the industries they service and with the products they sell. They know which companies are good and which are not so good. They must be aware of who has problems, who's on the move, where the new products are coming from, etc. They also must know their competition. Their continuing success depends on updated industry knowledge.

Referral through community service organizations

In most communities, you'll find that the "doers"—the people-oriented people—belong to such organizations as Rotary, Kiwanis, Lions, Elks, Jay Cee's, Optimists, Masons, and Shriners. The officers of these organizations are frequently an excellent referral source or know people in their business communities who are. Conversations at the meetings of such organizations frequently include inquiries concerning talented people.

Referral through professional organizations

Your friends, executives in your company, and even your competitors will be able to give you the names of professional organizations active in the industries of interest to you. Some of these organizations put out industry career development packets. Their officers are excellent information sources and referral leads.

Referral through local speaking groups

Aspiring managers and executives are always trying to improve their verbal skills. These people are excellent sources of ideas and contacts. Why not join such a group? You have nothing to lose.

Media sources

Newspapers, journals, tabloids, magazines, and company-disseminated information are all excellent sources for the names and titles of executives. In this connection, don't forget referral through those who write for and publish sources.

The above examples contain just a few of my ideas. Why not try some imaginative approaches of your own in this regard?

Below are some suggested scenarios for getting your foot in the door. You might try one, several, or all of these methods, or even a combination. Decide which one appeals to you and then use it.

The direct call to the decision maker

Call the decision maker to arrange for a consulting interview. The conversation might go as follows:

Scenario 1

> YOU: Could I please speak with _____ ?
> SECRETARY: I'm sorry, but he's very busy right now. Could I have him return your call?

Obviously, the decision maker is busy; otherwise, he wouldn't be in that position. All too frequently, decision makers use the "secretary hustle" to avoid having any additional demands made on their time. However, if you're overly courteous and cooperative, chances are that you'll wait and wait . . . and wait. Be assertive. Say, "Thanks, but I'm very busy as well. Could you please suggest a good time for me to call?" (Be sure to leave your name.) If the same thing happens again, ask for another time. *Persist!* It's surely better than playing that waiting game, and you will get results.

Once you have the decision maker on the line, you might say something like:

> "I understand that you're the decision maker regarding the _____ department. I'm very interested in getting some information about your company and that department."

or

> "I'm interested in getting some information about your company because I'm looking for a position."

or

> "If you would meet with me to discuss your company, you may find that I can identify areas in which I can contribute substantially."

Of course, as soon as you say anything about a job with the company, up go the red flares and the detour signs. The immediate response (almost a conditioned one) will be, "I'll be happy to switch you over to our personnel department. They'll give you all the information you need."

Now the most important commandment in your search efforts: *Thou shalt deal only with the decision maker.* How do you handle this problem? Try something like the following:

> "Sure, but will they tell me about you? Do they really know you? You're the top person in this department. Getting to know what kind

of person you are will show me whether *I'm* interested and what kind of potential I might have in your company and in this industry. Personnel departments don't tell me about the personality and character of your company, and I'm sure you'll agree that this is a very important consideration. When can we meet?"

Scenario 2

"Let's be honest with each other. I understand that you're a very busy executive. You don't have time to play games with personnel. Prior to accepting my present position, I learned the importance of meeting personally with the decision maker. Like you, I want to get things done. That's why I called you.

Scenario 3

For some time now, executive recruiters have been talking with me about opportunities in this industry.

Approach A

"Because I find myself at an important crossroads in my career—I'm about to accept a major promotion with my present employer—I feel it's important to get some additional input."

or

Approach B

"Several companies have recently made me offers. I really don't think that I've gotten enough exposure or gained enough knowledge to make an informed decision."

Either way

"Could we meet for about half an hour on Wednesday—say, 10:30— or Thursday during the lunch hour at your office?"

Following are some examples of techniques which could be considered a little out of line, though you might want to use them.

EXAMPLE 1 *(Overdoing it):* Call and make an appointment to discuss some company problems and some possible solutions that you feel could help the decision maker and the company.

EXAMPLE 2 *(Slightly overdoing it):* Call and make an appointment to meet with the decision maker for breakfast or cocktails because you need some help with a problem—your career. Suggest a place near the decision maker's office, and be sure to pick up the tab.

Scenario 4

Call and say that the decision maker's name was referred to you by a stockbroker, an employee, or a friend, for example.

> Tell the truth.
>
> "_____ said that you are a fine, knowledgeable, and helpful person. I was wondering whether I could have an hour of your time—say, next Tuesday at 5:30 or 5:45 or on Wednesday morning at 7:30 or 7:45."
>
> Always offer alternatives; it's only courteous, and it shows your savvy.

The hustle: it's not a dance

The commonest and easiest reply to any request for an executive's time is "Well, I'm very busy now, but perhaps Mrs. _____ can help you." Probably this is true, but that's not your problem. Your problem is to get in to see that decision maker. And so, press on:

> "Yes, I understand you're very busy. That's why I've suggested that we meet before or after business hours. I have some very important and specific questions to ask, and the answers are of major concern to me and my future. It really means a lot to me."

and/or

> "I know that you are the person with the most knowledge and experience in the department. My questions can be answered by only one person—you. I promise this won't be a waste of your time. Perhaps you might suggest a good time and place?"

The hustle: part two

"I just can't seem to get past that secretary." This is a common complaint. Remember that most secretaries leave at five on the dot. Get the executive's direct number from the switchboard operator and call about ten or fifteen minutes after business hours. You'll get through, and he or she probably won't be quite so harassed at that time. The decision maker might even be glad to hear a pleasant and sincere voice on the other end of the line.

The hustle: the final bump

You may call and be told, "If you're looking for a job, there's nothing available." Try something like the following:

> "That's why I want to meet with you. I know that if you needed someone, you'd call your personnel department or a search firm or

place an ad in the paper. The reason I want to meet with you is to find out *why* you don't need top talent? This industry has some outstanding potential for growth and profits. I'd like to meet with you to talk about this."

or

"That's why I want to meet with you. I'm very surprised that a company like yours, moving at the rate it's moving and with a product line like yours, isn't looking for an outstanding talent, one with proved abilities. That's why I want to meet with you. How about 7:30 at ——————— ?"

As a last resort you might mention a few things you feel you could contribute to the firm, but only if it's absolutely necessary. Don't try to conduct an interview over the phone.

Some words of counsel: Successful executives have well-developed egos. They like to think of themselves as very important and very "with it." You should be aware of this and use it to your own advantage. Find out what the decision maker's "hot buttons" are. Don't ever start the conversation with negatives or problems—this just doesn't work.

A final scenario

"I'm a ——————— [a position two or three levels below the decision maker's]. I'm at a very crucial point in my life. I have reformulated my goals, and I'm not quite sure how to achieve them or what path to take. I can't go to my own boss or to other executives in my own company because I'm not quite sure I want to stay there. I've read some interesting articles about you and your company, and I've spoken with some of your people. They've told me that you're a very understanding person. Because of that and because of the position you have, I'd like to meet with you. I'm sure that sometime during your life you were at a similar crossroads and needed an expert's advice. You know how much it would have helped. Now I need an expert to help me. Could you spare a half hour on Thursday night or Friday morning?"

Whenever you set an appointment, always make it for at least half an hour but allow for as much as an hour, though never more. You'll probably need that much time.

"Speaking of their time, how about mine?"

If you do as I suggest—select three to five industries and five companies in each industry—you will spend a lot of time being interviewed and setting up interviews. I'm also telling you to avoid being unemployed at all costs. How can you set up interviews when you're supposed to be working?

You've already seen that it's best to arrange interviews either before or after business hours. However, some executives will be willing to see you at coffee-break time or during business hours. How do you handle that one?

You can suddenly have a number of appointments with your dentist or your doctor, or your spouse can need your help in an emergency (be sure he or she knows about it), for example. These are relatively legitimate reasons for getting out of the office. And of course a vacation, if properly planned, can give you the time you need for interviewing.

"I object!" you say. "I just don't have the time to do all this." Yes, it is time-consuming, but can you honestly afford *not* to make this effort? If you take a little extra time and conduct your search the first time, you will avoid missing out on what could have been the opportunity of your lifetime.

The effort you make is for *you*, so that you can take advantage of your gifts, abilities, and skills and be appreciated for your talents, for your willingness to contribute, and—most important of all—for being yourself. Take the time to make this happen!

Another objection

"But," you say, "the industries and companies I've chosen require that all applicants, no matter who they are, be channeled through the personnel department."

Remember that during your *initial*, informal interviews, you aren't an applicant! You are merely gathering information so that when you are ready to make a decision, it will be an informed one, based on knowledge you've acquired as a result of your consulting interviewing efforts.

If you arrange to have your contacts personally refer and introduce you to the people you want to see, you will be able to bypass the personnel department.

No more objections, please

That's enough objections. Now you are starting to procrastinate. The real problem at this point might be that you've never done anything like this before. You wonder what will happen if you make a mistake and blow the whole thing. Well, believe me, your whole world won't come to an end. If you're ever going to be a successful manager or decision maker or if you're going to continue up the career ladder, you're going to have to make those mistakes and win those successes. Leadership requires sticking your neck out—*moving forward.* So, no matter what your personality type, the effort you make now will provide you with valuable experience in taking the initiative and going ahead.

To be a successful manager requires initiative, empathy, ego drive, persistence, and determination. But most important, leadership requires demonstrating your ability to motivate people—to get them to work *with* you. All these important fundamentals are part of the consulting interview.

How management's needs are served by the consulting interview

Chances are that by the time you've read this book, savvy managers will have read it as well. They'll know what's going on. Therefore, you might not have much difficulty arranging such an interview, and here's why.

Decision makers stand to profit as much as you do from the consulting interview, perhaps more. When it comes to recruiting, interviewing, and selecting people for their company (or division or department), they have problems.

Problem 1. Decision makers get bored—in fact, frustrated

Good managers must have a readily available pool of talent. Assembling this pool in the usual manner is boring and frustrating. If an opening has occurred and there is no one to promote from within, you're assisting with this responsibility. You're also giving the decision maker the opportunity to upgrade his or her staff. If you were a manager, how would you feel about an industrious, sincere, concerned person who came to seek your counsel and advice? You would want to know more about this person, wouldn't you?

Your interviewing executives is a pleasant departure for them. If you properly design and arrange your questions, you will be stroking their egos as you gain knowledge, advice, and counsel. This is anything but boring to them.

Problem 2. Decision makers become negative and skeptical

Like you, decision makers hate résumés, all of which seem to say the same thing. Résumés give them a headache and make them skeptical. During the consulting interview, you're gaining exposure for yourself and providing the executive with a sounding board. Your concern about the future of the company and the industry and this personal contact and effort are truly unique and exceptional. Your approach is something fresh and, in most cases, unknown to them—and they don't have to read a résumé. By introducing reality and pleasantries into your search, both role playing and tension can be reduced to a minimum.

Problem 3. Decision makers hate this part of their job

Decision makers don't like to "play God." They recognize that there is a human being behind each résumé. They truly don't want to make a mistake. But what can anybody really tell from a résumé anyway? And yet résumés are just about all that these people are given to work with, and *they hate it.* Your personal appearance and efforts are an easy, pleasant, and unique alternative.

Consulting interviews can provide decision makers with a prescreened, prequalified, and knowledgeable supply of talent (*if* you've done your homework and preparation). Additionally, the consulting interview means that decision makers don't need to worry about incurring the wrath of their competitors by recruiting from among them. They don't have to recruit—you're coming to them.

Problem 4. Decision makers know this part of their job takes time, effort, and money

The time you cost them will be pleasantly spent, and you won't take any money out of their budget. Want ads cost money, and who really looks at them anyway except unhappy and unemployed people?

Speaking of money, agency fees can run to 25 percent or more of the first year's income. Executive search fees commonly run in excess of 30 percent. The consulting interview is more than worth the time and effort—$5,000 to $25,000 or more—for both you and the decision makers. Here's why. Using the old method:

1. They must write up job descriptions.
2. They must write up people descriptions.
3. They must communicate their needs and requirements to the personnel department or to agencies, newspapers, etc. (Have you ever played the game "Pass It On"? You tell

your neighbor something, who in turn tells it to someone else, and so on. After three or four exchanges, there's little resemblance to the original story. Need I say more?)

4. They'll probably have to do a salary survey.
5. Perhaps a number of trips are required. With this method, you've come to them.
6. When placing ads, dealing with agencies, etc., they must worry about all the rules and regulations connected with discrimination.
7. They have to deal with people who are looking for "anything," as long as it's a job, and with unqualified people.
8. They have no guarantee, even after they do all this, that the hired candidate will feel more responsibility toward them than toward the employment agency counselor.
9. They have to develop and use a number of recruitment sources—agencies, college placement offices, technical and trade associations, and so on. That takes time, effort, and money.

***Problem 5. Decision makers have a
personnel manager to do this***

The old methods just don't work efficiently or effectively. Eighty percent of the work force is underemployed, 8 percent is unemployed, people under thirty-five change jobs on the average of once every $1^1/_2$ years, and those over thirty-five do so once every three years.[1] These statistics are incredible! Even large companies using the latest hiring techniques experience a 30 percent error in their hiring efforts.

Additionally, decision makers have to deal with many agencies and search firms that are unwilling to speak with the personnel department. You are offering something different—you're not selling anything. You're coming in as an equal, a professional; you are prepared and are asking intelligent questions. What an incredible relief!

In essence, then, the consulting interview reduces—perhaps eliminates—decision makers' dependence on a department and a concept that have proved ineffective.

Because of all these negatives, most executives will wait until there is an opening before they start looking. This is not only expensive and inefficient but also a very serious breach of their

[1]Statistics from Richard N. Bolles, *What Color Is Your Parachute? A Practical Manual for Job-Hunters and Career-Changers,* rev. ed., Ten Speed Press, Berkeley, Calif., 1977, preface. Used by permission of the author.

responsibility. Open territories, open positions—all are voids which competition loves and thrives upon.

"But what if they still won't see me?"

One question has been bothering you: "What happens if I do all this work and preparation, only to discover that the S.O.B. I want to meet won't cooperate and give me an interview?" There are only four logical things to do in this case:
1. Ask yourself what you did right. Did you do anything wrong?
2. Ask yourself whether you had enough persistence and determination. Perhaps the decision maker is testing you to see how far you'll go—to see whether you're really interested.
3. Get mad! Repeat the reasons for your concern and use your anger to reinforce it (when all else fails, that is).
4. Recognize that the decision maker blew the chance to meet the "fantastic you" and share some great war stories.

Obviously, that decision maker is selfish and self-centered and has lost again. Now the competition has the advantage and the opportunity. Futhermore, you don't want to work for that kind of person anyway.

Another step in the right direction

Remember that if you are what you think you are, if you can do what you think you can do, if you can contribute the way you think you can, and if you can communicate this to the decision maker, there is a good chance that he or she will seriously consider upgrading the staff to make room for a real winner.

The importance of timing

Here is another important commandment: *Thou shalt not wait for the right time; thou shalt make the time right.* A good explanation for this commandment can be found in the following quotations:

> Most people wait until everything is "just right" before they "do anything." They refuse to go out on a limb because they don't understand that the fruit is always on the limb.

The person who waits until all the lights are on green before he "starts" will never leave home. He ends up being a "never doer." In reality, it does not take much of a man—or much of a woman—to succeed and be happy, but it does take all of him or all of her.[2]

Timing for positions you wish to create

The holiday season—a bad time for interviewing? Late spring and early summer, just before people go on vacation—another bad time for interviewing? Right? *Wrong!*

Many companies operate on a fiscal-year basis, and others on a calendar-year basis. Their budgets and their hiring considerations are planned around these periods. The fact that a position isn't available right now doesn't mean that one won't be available next week or next month. But there's an even better possibility that, as a result of your exposure, a position might be made available when the new budget comes through.

Yes, late fall, the holiday season, late spring, and early summer are bad times in terms of hiring, but *these are the best times* in terms of exposure—in terms of laying the groundwork for positions that will be created in two or three months.

Timing for positions open now or becoming available

There is no good or bad time here. Management is continually replacing and upgrading talent. Let's look at the problems management faces in its replacement responsibilities:

Death
Terminations
Transfers
Retirement
Disabilities
Serious illnesses
People quitting
Hiring errors
Upgrading of talent
Maternity leaves

Again, your exposure and follow-up are of continuing importance. If you've "clicked"—if you've found the right position—go after it.

[2]Zig Ziglar, in John Hammond (ed.), *The Fine Art of Doing Better*, Los Angeles, 1974, pp. 105–106. Author's royalties donated to Junior Achievement, Inc.

You're hardheaded—you still don't like the idea

I want to remind you that unless you get out and do something—eliminate the "I can'ts"—you'll never achieve your goals. The methods of the consulting interview I've outlined here are meant to produce results and even to bring a reasonable amount of pleasure to you and the decision maker. But I can do only so much to convince you of the effectiveness of this technique. If you are modest, unaggressive, and soft-spoken, the idea of a consulting interview may seem totally foreign to you. Remember, however, that professional flexibility and openness to change are critically important.

If, after all this, you adamantly refuse even to consider the consulting interview, here's your alternative: I strongly suggest that you do everything outlined and explained up to the beginning of this chapter—setting goals, doing research, and so on. Then go through the "personnel shuffle." If you do get in the door to see the decision maker, take it from Chapter 10—on.

You're in New York, and they're somewhere else

Do you remember the commandment concerned with meeting the decision maker *in person*? Near or far, you must go where the decision maker is. This will cost you money, but I promise you that it's well worth it. (Incidentally, costs of searching for employment in the same line of work are tax-deductible.) In fact, if you handle it properly, decision makers will make special time available for you because you have come a long distance to meet with them personally. Also, you will have the opportunity to visit other companies and decision makers in the area.

You can arrange for an interview with a company in a distant location over the phone, of course, but you can also send a letter, *but only if necessary* and *only as a last resort*. The following are examples of such letters:

> Dear Mr. _____ :
> Over the past five years I've been employed either part or full time in the _____ industry with the _____ company. This experience has provided me with substantial exposure to the products of your company. My family as well as I have been involved in the _____ business for many years, and I look forward to continuing this association, but with the finest company—yours.

Below are a few of the contributions I have been able to make while employed at _____ :

1. I have shown a desire and ability for growth within the _____ industry. I started employment with _____ as a _____, determined that I was going to be the best _____ in the store. The manager acknowledged my achievements and I was promoted to _____. Later I received training in the _____ department. One summer, I was asked to act as manager in charge of the department twice a week. I progressed as far as possible as a part-time, temporary employee.

2. I worked hard to achieve excellence in all _____ operations. I've received two _____ performance reports since I've been employed with _____ and was awarded 100 points out of a possible 100 in both instances.

3. As a result of my proved record of performance, I've been trained for various positions in the _____ and have always been immediately rehired when seeking summer employment.

4. All _____ supervisors under whom I have worked have complimented me on my work and dependability.

But more important than what I've done in the past is what I can do for your company on a continuing basis in the future, if given the opportunity. Here are some of the unique contributions I feel I can make to your company:

1. I have proved knowledge and experience in the _____ industry as a result of my affiliation with _____. Not only have I stocked, displayed, and sold a wide variety of consumer products, but I have also dealt on a one-to-one basis with the purchasers of these products.

2. I am success-motivated and goal-oriented. I strive to excel and am not satisfied with being just mediocre. Setting goals is and has been an essential part of my life for as long as I can remember.

3. I recognize the necessity for personal contact and other important elements in the sale of consumer products. I've spent two years selling _____ on a full-time basis. During those two years, I spent in excess of sixty hours a week making personal contacts and selling in what constitutes, for our company, one of the toughest markets in the world.

4. I understand and realize the importance of doing that little extra something to assure success, whether in closing a sale or carrying out any task which I'm assigned.

5. I am *career*-oriented. I'm not just seeking a job—I already have a job. I want a position which will provide a career opportunity in the _____ industry. I want a position which will help me to use my background and education in the fields of marketing and sales.

Though my wife and I currently reside in _____, we are willing to relocate anywhere and would be happy to live in any area in which I can make the greatest contribution, given my talents and qualifications.

I feel very confident that if I am afforded the opportunity, your company could benefit substantially from our mutual affiliation. The final decision is up to you, of course. I will travel to _____ on _____ and would sincerely appreciate the opportunity to spend half an hour with you. I'll be calling you in approximately one week to confirm this.

Sincerely,

Dear Mrs. _____ :

In today's highly complex and constantly changing business environment, the only thing certain about the future is change itself. Those individuals and businesses which are quickly able to adapt to this changing atmosphere will succeed, while those which are not able to cope will fail.

Foretelling the future without the use of a crystal ball can be extremely hazardous, but examining current trends and events and projecting them into probable future happenings is most necessary for the continued growth of enterprises in the challenging and more competitive business environment that lies ahead. It demands the use of the most advanced methods of management and control techniques to devise innovative procedures that will reduce waste and inefficiency. I believe that I possess the special and sought-after talents necessary to do this.

I am a CPA, MBA (accounting), and I have the highest professional competence in the highly technical fields of finance, accounting, and taxes. My ability to adapt these technical skills to business is what separates me from other financial executives. I have the unique ability to comprehend complex business transactions quickly and to see the forest through the accounting trees.

Besides my high technical competence, my attributes include leadership ability, the ability to motivate people, adaptability, strong decision-making ability, energetic and aggressive enthusiasm, and the perseverance to see that my predetermined goals and objectives are achieved. My professional philosophies are concerned with integrity, initiative, and loyalty and dedication to my employer.

I am very confident that I can make major and significant contributions to your company, as I have to my previous employers. More specifically, here are some of the contributions I've made in previous positions:

1. Designed and implemented an integrated management information system which increased efficiency and operating margins
2. Designed and implemented a production information and control system with MRP which reduced inventory by 40 percent and delivery time by three weeks

3. Significantly streamlined accounting procedures, allowing relevant information to be available on a current basis, with a significant reduction in personnel and outside accounting expenses
4. Created significant tax savings to the company with tax planning, conversion to the LIFO method of inventory valuation, and favorable negotiated settlements of long-standing tax cases
5. Significantly increased investment income through the proper timing and allocation of investments

I firmly believe that accounting and finance should be used as a tool in the forefront of business decisions and not as an afterthought (hindsight) critique of operations. I feel that the accounting and systems areas of most companies are very good at collecting data but that their inability to collect only *significant data* is what frequently makes them unnecessarily expensive and nonresponsive to management's needs. My thorough understanding of business gives me the ability to design systems which collect only relevant and pertinent data on a timely basis for management decision making.

In addition to the usual management and financial skills expected of an individual who has achieved the successes I have, I feel that I have other unique skills and abilities that will benefit your organization:

1. The ability to identify areas of waste and inefficiency and potential problem areas and to recommend and *implement* the correct solutions
2. The proved ability to define meaningful objectives, evaluate alternatives, and develop a plan with precise and objective standards for measuring and monitoring operations
3. An extraordinary ability to communicate and motivate key company personnel to maximum efficiency
4. The proved ability to create a financial plan by identifying trends within the company and by forecasting the general business outlook for the entire industry, as a result of taking into account the probable effect of anticipated political events and governmental policies and programs
5. The proved ability to identify innovative methods for achieving corporate goals and objectives, especially financial goals such as acquiring capital

I strive for financial professionalism. My unique abilities, as proved by my previous successes, make me a very rare talent. My training, knowledge, and experience will allow me to contribute almost immediately to your company's bottom line. My knowledge and strong business acumen could make me a valuable addition to your management team.

I will be flying to _____ on _____ to meet with several companies in your area. I would sincerely appreciate meeting with you for about one hour and will be calling you in advance to arrange a mutually convenient time.

Sincerely,

Commentary

I'm sure that after reading these letters, you said, "That sure is an awful lot of self-praise." Well, if *you* don't brag about yourself, who do you think is going to?

Yes, these letters are strong and hard-hitting. They have to be. The meek will inherit the bad jobs; the strong and hard-hitting executives will run the companies. I may have overstated my case a bit, but I have done so in order to push you a little bit further toward honestly representing yourself and your potential to contribute.

SIX

Designing Your Niche

Make your carving mistakes now

To gain relevant knowledge about the industries, companies, and decision makers that you are interested in, you have to make personal contacts and ask questions. We have seen that the best way to do this is through the informal consulting interview.

But you must be careful. Practice makes perfect. So make all (or most of) your real blunders with a few decision makers in companies that you are least interested in. Then target your efforts where they will be most productive.

What will you ask each of these people? What are they going to ask you? Specifically, why do you even want to get together with them? These are just a few of the important questions that you must answer before you go after the big game. Let's discuss this in detail.

Purposes of the practice interview

One or two practice interviews will give you the following experience:

1. You will make your mistakes with companies of lesser importance to you; then, with the ones that count, you will be able to handle yourself knowledgeably and effectively.

2. You will see how you react in an interview situation of this type.
3. You will have the opportunity to compare industries, companies, and decision makers.
4. You will see how well you have prepared yourself—how your questions work, whether you've left anything out, etc.

A word of reassurance

During all your interviewing efforts, be aware that the decision makers will respect the confidential nature of these meetings and will not, in any way, jeopardize your present position.

The right questions

In my years of experience, I've found that one of the hardest things to get job candidates to do is to ask questions. Why is this? Perhaps they are afraid that if they ask questions, they might be doing some of the following:
1. Alienating the interviewer
2. Taking too much of the interviewer's time
3. Disclosing a lack of knowledge regarding the industry or the specific company
4. Asking stupid questions

Obviously, the secret to overcoming these fears is to write down your questions in advance. Get away from them for a few hours and then go back and review them. If some of them don't seem right, either reword them or discard them. It's that simple.

If you don't ask questions and if you don't acquire all the information you need before you are hired, you are apt to make some very unpleasant discoveries about your employer (and vice versa) after you're hired.

There is no such thing as a stupid question

There are some questions which might be considered inappropriate or out of line, but not stupid. By preparing your questions before the interview, researching your chosen companies and industries, and acquiring as much information as possible about the decision makers in these companies, you'll reduce the possibility of asking inappropriate questions to a minimum.

When you do ask questions, try to ask as many open-ended ones as possible. Many answers to your *specific* questions are available in financial information sources or are reserved for the actual interview situation, the *formal* interview.

Remember that unless you ask questions, you'll never get answers. I've often had people tell me that they felt complimented because I'd asked them questions and that they had truly enjoyed the exchange. If you are afraid that a question might come across improperly but would really like to have an answer, you might preface it with one of the following comments: "I'm not sure how to go about asking this question, but—"or "This might not be the time or place to ask this question, but I've tried unsuccessfully to find out the answer, and so—"

By questioning someone, you are relieving that person of the burden of questioning you and conducting the interview—you're the one who's directing it. Also, when you ask for decision makers' counsel and advice, in essence you are stroking their egos. You are asking them to talk about themselves, their lives, and their work—and they love it. In that kind of situation, they're trying to help and inform you (perhaps even impress you). How's that for a turnabout in an interview situation? And this turnabout is truly fair play!

A final thought

What happens if you ask inappropriate questions during your practice interviews? That's what practice is all about. You aren't expected to be completely knowledgeable about the interviewer's company. If you were, you'd be in the interviewer's shoes.

And so, two more commandments: *Thou shalt learn to formulate and ask questions*, and, the secret to being a good listener, *Thou shalt never offer answers to questions which you might ask of a person.*

Questions to answer yourself— before the interview

It is important for you to be well informed about the industry of your choosing and about specific companies within it *before the interview!*

Be advised that the following list of questions is far from complete. It is meant merely to get you started. You must add as many others as you can think of. Answer the questions in detail. Where applicable, add the question "Why?" after your answer. This will give you additional insights.

Industry questions

1. Is the industry large enough to enable you to grow within it? (For example, is there more than one company?) Will it be? How soon?
2. Is the industry in a growing or declining stage of transition or change?
3. How much of the industry is government-controlled, government-related, or government-regulated? Is there any anticipation of change in this regard?
4. How much of the industry is completely controlled by one giant and thus monopolized accordingly?
5. Is the industry so small that all your efforts would be "missionary work" (i.e., going out to create needs)? If so, do you really identify with that kind of effort?
6. Who are the biggest companies in the industry, and what are their respective positions?
7. Is your personality compatible with this type of industry and position?
8. Do you really identify with the industry and its products and with the people in it?
9. What is the potential of the industry?
10. Why are you specifically interested in this industry?
11. Are the products of this industry subject to competition of a cutthroat and destructive nature?
12. Where will this industry be in five years? Ten years?
13. Is there already too much competition within this industry?

General company questions

Company Location

1. Is the company located in a geographically desirable area?
2. Will relocation be required of you and your family?
3. If so, how will this affect your children and their education?
4. Will the commuting be excessive?
5. How does your family feel about relocation?
6. Is the company location relatively unimportant to any position you might have in mind (e.g., outside sales, in

which little personal contact with the company is required)?

Company Products
1. Do you identify with the products or services?
2. Do you believe in them?
3. Are the products competitive as to price? Design? Packaging? Quality? Effectiveness?
4. Will competing companies soon be offering new and better
   products?
5. What are the product names and descriptions?
6. How about new products or services?

Company Size
1. Is the company so large that you will get lost in it, or is that
   your objective? (Only you can gauge this.)
2. Is the company large enough to provide you with the
   breadth of training and experience that you seek?
3. Is the company so large that the training and experience
   you receive will be too limited and specific and you will be
   given no latitude to express and develop yourself?
4. Conversely, is the company so small that the things which
   will be required of you are beyond your capabilities, which
   will result in frustration and expectations of you beyond
   your abilities and experience?

Company People
1. Are they your kind of people?
2. Is the company so large that you will be just a number, not
   a person?

Company Growth
1. Is the company growing and increasing its market-share
   percentage, maintaining the status quo, or losing its
   share?

Specific company questions
1. Is the company publicly owned? Privately owned?
2. Is the company a parent? A division? A subsidiary?
3. Who are the top executives in the company?
4. What are some important facts concerning company
   history, recent acquisitions, etc.?
5. What is the state of the company's financial health?

6. What specifically is the company's position in the industry? Is it gaining or losing?
7. What are some of the major problems which the company might be facing now, has recently faced, or will be facing in the near future?
8. If the company is publicly owned, what stock exchange is it traded on? What is its symbol? What is the present price of the stock? What is the company's P/E ratio? (You can get excellent information regarding a privately owned company by looking at the financial sheets of its competitors and drawing comparisons accordingly.)
9. If the company is publicly owned and traded on one of the major exchanges, what is the stock's most recent history? Up? Down? Sideways?
10. Is the stock overvalued or undervalued, and why?[1]
11. What is the company's recent sales performance? How does this compare with past performance? What does this mean for the future? How does this relate to the recent sales performance of other companies in the industry?
12. What are the company's short-term and long-term financial prospects?
13. What are some of the *unique* things about the company's sales, products, marketing programs, methods of production and distribution, etc.? Why are these unique? Why are they successful?
14. Does the company provide an initial training program? Is it extensive and effective? Are there ongoing training programs? Are they extensive and effective?
15. In what stage of the corporate growth cycle is the company?
16. Does the company have a good name and reputation?

Questions about yourself

1. Why are you personally and professionally interested in this company and its products and/or services?
2. Why are you having an interview with this person (in detail)?

---

[1]Companies with high P/E ratios frequently dominate an industry or even monopolize it. That's the reason for excellent earnings and growth, two of the important factors to investors. Your concern here is whether this domination or monopolization of the industry will continue. How close is the market to saturation with the product, etc.?

3. Will the position you are seeking require that you be near top management (the "action") in order to achieve your goals for growth and promotion, or is the action in the field, the production area, or somewhere else?
4. Do you know how you are going to present yourself and how you are going to handle the interview?
5. Where are you in your professional development and growth?
6. Do you have the background and abilities necessary to really help a company grow or turn itself around?
7. If you still have a lot to learn about growth, industry fundamentals, etc., where should you be targeting your efforts?
8. Can you foresee happiness for yourself in this company and in this industry?
9. Do you think you'll be able to use and develop your skills and talents to the maximum in this company? Your initiative? Your imagination? Your common sense? Your knowledge? Your experience?
10. Are you becoming a corporate nonentity?
11. Are you utilizing your education?
12. Are you doing the "right thing" in the "right industry" in the "right company" and at the "right time"?
13. Are you utilizing your unique skills and abilities?
14. Are you growing, personally and professionally, on a continuing basis?
15. Are you able to express yourself?
16. Are your opinions respected and sought after?
17. Have you exhausted all the possible opportunities with your current employer?

You may be thinking that this last listing should be the longest one. After all, who you are, what you can do, and how you can contribute are possibly the most important considerations and must be covered in depth. Well, you're right. Chapters 9 and 12 will do this.

The "right" decision maker

In Chapter 2 we placed a great deal of emphasis on getting rid of everybody and everything which history has proved to be ineffective in a job search. These things lead to frustration and to a tremendous waste of your precious time and effort.

In this connection, perhaps the reason you are continually

running into roadblocks in your job hunt is that *You have improperly identified the decision maker.* We have seen that the finest information source regarding an industry, a company, and a position is a decision maker. But you have to find the right one, and sometimes this isn't easy.

How to identify the right decision maker

First, don't be afraid to go to the top; as a rule of thumb, remember that the decision maker is the boss of your boss-to-be. Why should you go after this person? Because it's always more advantageous and effective to be referred down, rather than up.

Second, some of the warmest and nicest people are at the top. They have arrived, and they have a lot to be proud of (so give them their due). They know how hard it was to get where they are. If you approach them properly, they'll respond to you with the help, counsel, and advice you need.

Next, start focusing on the position you would be best suited to fill. Determine which person in the management hierarchy would be your boss. Identify that person and his or her boss; then seek out an opportunity to interview the latter.

Additional concerns

In deciding on the position you would be best suited for, be very careful in your self-appraisal. Once you've carefully identified and established your ability to perform, you just might be pleasantly surprised to find that the position you initially identified is one or two levels below the level at which you'll best be able to function. Don't be afraid to set your sights high.

Seeking out the boss of your boss-to-be can prove confusing because power structures vary greatly from one company to another. For example, in Company X, all hiring decisions, no matter what, might be made solely by the company president—*that* person is the decision maker. In Company Y, however, which is the same size and has the same dollar volume, etc., hiring decisions and responsibilities are vested in the hands of each immediate superior. Here your *boss-to-be* is the decision maker.

The following signals will tell you that you're not dealing with the *true* decision maker:
1. *Frustration*
2. Disappointments
3. Put-offs
4. Problems with communication

If you are encountering these problems, you'd better reevaluate your strategy. You have made a tactical error and have spent all your time and effort on a person who doesn't have the power to help you get the position you want with this company.

In short, be very careful and don't *assume* anything. Ask questions before you put your foot in your mouth or waste a lot of time and effort. Let's repeat that all-important commandment: *Thou shalt not deal with anyone but the decision maker.*

How can you be sure you have identified the right person for your efforts? You can do this by asking questions. In Chapter 5, we identified a large number of referral sources. You should ask them whether the person you are going to meet has hiring authority for the position that interests you. If so, great! But if not, either try another route (referral) to the top or try to get a referral from this decision maker to a higher level.

Here are a few examples for those of you who might choose to go the direct route.

Example 1: You're seeking a national sales managerial position. Call and ask the company switchboard operator for the names of the president of the company and the vice president in charge of sales and marketing. This information can be acquired from brokerage firm information sheets, annual reports, etc. I suggest calling the company for such information because there is so much turnover in many industries today that financial information sheets are sometimes outdated.

Example 2: You're seeking a production managerial position. Call and ask the switchboard operator for the name of the person who is in charge of production for the company; be sure to get his or her title as well. You might even go so far as to ask the name and title of this person's boss. In short, try to glean as much information as possible during that phone conversation.[2]

Of course, just getting names isn't enough. How do you go about acquiring information about the decision maker personally and professionally? Remember that knowledge is your ammunition.

Acquiring information about the decision maker

To help you overcome any anxiety you might feel about meeting a decision maker for the first time, it is a good idea to do some research regarding this person—to gain knowledge (ammunition)

[2]In these two examples you can again see the value of being referred.

that will enable you to speak with him or her as an equal and from a position of strength.

Ask questions such as the following while doing your research, while gathering together information about the company and the industry, and perhaps during your conversations with people who are in some way related to the company or decision maker:

1. Could you tell me something about him personally and professionally?
2. What is his background and education?
3. What knowledge and experience does he have?
4. What are his interests?
5. What are his likes and dislikes?
6. Does he have any claims to fame?
7. Could you tell me something about specific problem areas he's concerned with in the company?

Such information can be helpful but difficult to acquire. You might have to meet again your reference source or someone closer to the decision maker. Once you've done this, make a listing like the following:

Company _____ Referred by _____
Decision maker _____
Title _____ In charge of _____

1. Important duties, responsibilities, and authorities:
2. Personality:
   a. Successes:
   b. Pet peeves:
   c. Interests:
   d. Likes:
   e. Dislikes:
   f. "Hot buttons" (turn-ons):
3. Background and experience:
4. Personal factors:
   a. Age:
   b. Place of birth:
   c. Family:
5. Personality type:

You can add questions to this list reflecting your own interests and concerns.

Once you have this information, you might even write a biographical sketch of the person. Either way, make sure that you have enough information. If you don't, try to get some more.

Practice how you plan to handle each decision maker. Ask

yourself how you would like to be handled if you were in his or her shoes.

The goal of this effort is to enable you to know all the decision makers you will be talking to before you ever meet them. This will help you to get over any anxiety you might feel and to approach these people from a number of different angles.

In Chapter 8 we shall go into the questions to be asked of the decision makers. First, however, we shall discuss a few additional concerns.

SEVEN

The Consulting Interview: Preparing for it

Setting the stage

Certain basics apply to all your interviewing efforts, formal and informal. Let's get these basics out of the way. Instead of assuming that you know all these things, I want to cover each one here, because each of these fundamentals and concerns is important. If you already know all this, please don't take offense; just stay with the program.

In this chapter and the following two, we shall continue to be concerned with informal interviewing techniques. Formal interviewing techniques are the subject of Chapter 10.

The basics

An important consideration in preparing for any interview is your personal appearance and the way you present (sell) yourself during the first three to four minutes. This first impression is what you'll be striving to confirm or disconfirm during the rest of that interview and during any interviews that may follow.

The physical you

Do you look the part? Do you look like the kind of person the company hires? Do your carriage, appearance, and attitude reflect success? Do you seem to belong in that environment? These things are part of the first impression you're striving to project—the impression that you've "got it together." This chapter will concentrate on the "physical you." Do you have what it takes? During the first few minutes, the interviewer will be trying to assess whether you have the right qualifications, experience, potential, and personality for the company. Let's discuss each of these individually.

Ability
1. Qualifications
   a. Have you worked for the right companies?
   b. Have you done the right things while with these companies?
   c. Have you progressed to the right levels within these companies?
2. Experience
   a. Have you supervised the right number of people and the right kinds of people?
   b. Where are you on your own ladder to success?
   c. Have you done any business development?
   d. Have you handled the appropriate types of business activities *and* with a proved record of success?

That's right—for the higher-level positions, it's not a question of "Can you?" but rather "Have you?" and "Have you done these things successfully?"

Attitude and character
1. Potential
   a. Will this change be a step up? A lateral step? A steppingstone?
   b. Can you progress from here?
   c. Will this be "it" for you—the job you'll retire from?
   d. Will you be able to take the decision maker's place some day?
2. Personality
   a. Will your personality fit in here?
   b. What is your self-image? What do you really think of yourself?
   c. Will there be friction, or will you come in and *earn* the respect of others in the organization? Will you stop, look, and listen, or will you be "a bull in a china shop"?
   d. Is this company—this position—"you"?

In short, this part of the first impression is concerned with your self-confidence!

Your personal appearance

Clothes

Look in the mirror and ask yourself, "How would I feel about me if I were interviewing me?" Look carefully; do you really look like an executive? Are you properly dressed?

Men should always wear a conservative business suit (sport jackets are a bit too casual), and the tie should not be too wild. It's difficult for an executive to be overdressed for an interview. Clothes should always be clean, neat, and pressed.

Women should always wear a conservative dress or a suit with a skirt. Pants suits are really not formal enough. Remember that executives must be well groomed. Watch for color coordination.

Hair

How about your hair? Is it neat and trim? For men, a neat, professional-looking haircut is always in line. Long hair is time-consuming, doesn't look tidy, and isn't conservative.

I've always found that women with long hair look a lot more professional if they wear it up. Short hair is fine.

Shoes

Are your shoes polished? Are they moderate in style? Conservative-looking shoes, properly polished, can't possibly hurt your chances. (Incidentally, white socks don't make it in the "pro" world.)

Toiletries and cosmetics

As with everything else, use good common sense here. Too much makeup, perfume, or after-shave lotion, for example, is a real turn-off for most people.

Cleanliness

Of course, men should have a clean shave. A daily bath and all those other things your Mom told you to do are important!

Miscellaneous

Bad breath: Breath mints or gum can help, but *don't* chew during the interview.

Smoking: Be careful here. You're better off forgetting about smoking during the interview and concentrating on the business at hand.

Drinking: Your behavior in this regard is loaded with meaning. If you are offered a drink, turn it down, even if the interviewer has one. If you have any alcohol on your breath, *forget the interview!*

Sex, religion, and politics: Watch it here. You have come to discuss a position and everything related to it. There isn't any time for these subjects. If the interviewer wants to discuss them, beg off and get the interview back on the right track.

Your body language

Smiling

Smile throughout the interview when it's called for. How can anyone possibly dislike a person who is smiling? Smiling is contagious. If the interviewer isn't someone who makes you feel like smiling, use this trick: Imagine that he or she weighs 300 pounds, is bald, has no clothes on, and is sitting on a toilet smoking a big cigar. Now, if that doesn't make you smile, try to think of something that will.

Eye contact

Look into the interviewer's eyes. Do this throughout the interview, even if the interviewer doesn't meet your gaze. Most people believe they're getting the straight scoop from someone who looks them in the eye. Eye contact is extremely important.

Posture

Don't slouch. Your posture will tell a great deal about you as a professional. It will also tell how you feel as the interview progresses. If the interview is tending in a negative direction and you start to sink lower into your chair, this says you're being intimidated. Do something about it! Sit up and look alive. You're dealing from a position of strength and equality. You're interviewing the decision maker, remember? Don't forget that you're selling yourself.

Your handshake

Avoid the "limp-fish" handshake and the "once-over-lightly" kind as well. But don't break a person's hand, either. When being introduced, a nice, firm, *sincere* handshake is proper and called for, whether you're meeting a woman or a man.

Your voice

Speak loudly enough to be heard and enunciate clearly. Speak directly to the interviewer so that he or she won't have to strain to hear you or ask you to repeat yourself.

Your hands

Don't fidget. Don't have your hands in your pockets and keep them away from your face. Don't fiddle with anything on the interviewer's desk; that's forbidden territory.

The interviewer's body language

That takes care of the basics for you. Now, what about understanding the decision maker's body language? The interviewer will be sending signals which can tell you more about what's really going on in his or her mind than all the things that are being verbalized. It's important for you to understand what this person is communicating physically.

Here are some things to watch for during the interview:

Some positives

Smiling and holding the chin: The interviewer is pleased and has decided in your favor.

Good eye contact: You have the interviewer's interest.

Changing positions: The interviewer has had a change of attitude (possibly good or bad).

Taking a deep breath or sitting back in the chair: The interviewer is sold on you. *Don't oversell!*

Holding the fingers together: The interviewer is confident of his or her control of the situation. You are not threatening.

Some negatives

Tapping the top of the desk: You're in trouble. Leave!

Folding the arms: The interviewer is defensive. He or she is turned off by you and is not interested.

Rubbing the nose: The interviewer feels resentful and disagrees with you.

Bad eye contact: This person has problems; it might be best to end the interview.

Raising one eyebrow: The interviewer doesn't believe you.

Looking at a watch, glancing at a clock, or accepting phone calls: You have lost the interviewer's interest. Wrap it up.

Don't monopolize the conversation

This is the decision maker's time to talk—to give advice and counsel. Say as little as possible and listen carefully. There are few people in the world who don't appreciate a good listener. You already know what you know. Now you want to learn what the decision maker knows. You're there for advice and counsel. By listening intently to what he or she says, you will gain an understanding of the opportunities that exist in the company and the industry. You will acquire the knowledge you need to carve your niche.

Other don'ts of the consulting interview (and all interviews)

1. Never arrange for an appointment or interview on a Monday morning or a Friday afternoon.
2. Don't knock anybody or anything—not even a company's competitors.
3. Don't bring up negatives; this should be a totally positive experience.
4. Don't bring this book and ask questions from it. (Write your questions on a piece of paper.)
5. Don't sit like a bump on a log as if you are waiting to be entertained.
6. Don't try to compete with the telephone. If a phone call interrupts the conversation, be courteous. After the interviewer has finished with the call, pick up where you left off.
7. Don't ever leave without exchanging business cards with the interviewer.
8. Don't bring a friend or your wife or husband along.
9. Don't give the impression that you are in desperate need of a job.

Bring your equipment

Before going to the interview, be sure you have the right equipment:

1. A pen and pencil. (If one doesn't work, the other will.)
2. A writing portfolio or tablet.
3. Your own set of questions written on a separate sheet of paper and inserted in the portfolio. (These should be easily readable and preferably typed.)

Be a doer, not a procrastinator

At this point, you may be running into the problems of procrastination. You aren't sure that you've gotten everything down pat, and you think you need more preparation before you take any real action. At this point, please remember that the anticipation is always worse than the realization. Get out and start your job hunt. You'll be pleasantly surprised with the results, and you'll be very glad that you did.

Here's a quotation (author unknown) that I'm fond of. You might like it too:

> It's not what you do, but how you do it that counts. It's what you do, not what you could do. Most always, you regret what you didn't do, not what you did do.

Let's see where we are

Now that you've done all your homework and your research, your apprenticeship is almost complete. You have studied your tools (your unique talents, skills, and abilities), your materials (the companies and industries of your choosing), and your objectives (your plans, goals, and dreams). They all seem to fit in with your likes and dislikes as well as your personality and your philosophy.

Now it's time to take your tools, materials, and objectives and start carving your niche. But first let's get that practice run—the informal consulting interview—out of the way before discussing the ones that really count.

EIGHT

The Consulting Interview: Conducting It

You have called and made the appointment, and within twenty-four hours of the time set for the interview you have confirmed it. You have become "professionally friendly" with the secretary. (Still, you must never use the decision maker's first name when calling.) You know where to go and how to get there. Now you're sitting in the outer office or in a restaurant. (Remember to shy away from bars.)

Like a speech, an interview should consist of three parts: the introduction, the body, and the conclusion. Let's discuss each of these.

The introduction

After the social amenities, *you* should begin the interview by saying something like:

> "First, I'd like to say how much I appreciate your taking time to meet with me. As I said when we first spoke, the reason I wanted to meet with you today is—. I've prepared a few questions that you might have the answers to."

or

"I'm sure you're probably wondering why I've asked you to meet with me. All too many people go through life looking inward, trying to learn from their own mistakes. I don't subscribe to that philosophy. I want to look outward, to learn to benefit from the successes of others, as well as my own. You've become successful in this industry, and I'd like to try to gain some insights into how you've been able to do this. I've prepared a few questions that you might help me with."

Be warm and sincere. If your attitude is formal, the interviewer will assume the managerial role. Remember that, for the most part, decision makers will act as you expect them to.

Caution

It's all too easy to talk about yourself, to bring up negative aspects of your present job and why you're not going anywhere there. Don't do it! Don't weaken. But, most important, don't introduce negatives about yourself or your future. This will serve to cloud your own thinking and very possibly might turn the interviewer off as well.

Let's look at some examples of this kind of approach. Then you can judge for yourself how it might work against you.

"Well, I've reached a plateau with my present employer. Rather than resigning my future to mediocrity there, I'm going to look for something with a real future."

or

"Because of the seemingly limited opportunities in my present job, I've decided to search out another company in which I can contribute."

or

"I'm doing a very fine job where I'm currently working, but there isn't enough challenge or opportunity for growth. I feel stagnated."

Don't statements like these introduce a little "gray" into the discussion? It's obvious that you're dissatisfied; otherwise, you wouldn't have arranged the meeting in the first place.

Here's a better approach:

"Your industry is one of five which I've identified as having tremendous potential for growth, presently and in the foreseeable future. That's why I wanted to meet with you—to get the straight scoop on what the future holds for your company. But more important, I'd like to find out what you consider to be some of your secrets for success in this industry."

or

"In doing research into your industry and this company, I've read articles that you've written and talked with people about you. I've heard nothing but good things. I'd like to know some of your secrets for success, such as how you've gotten to where you are today. In short, enlighten me—tell me about yourself."

Another caution

I almost hesitate to include this, but don't ask anything about the decision maker's mistakes. These are none of your business, and you want to concentrate on positives—the reasons for his or her success.

The body

Once the decision maker has started expounding on his or her ideas and successes, you, of course, must guide the interview with the proper questions at the proper time. You are seeking the decision maker's cooperation. The more empathy you show and the more rapport you can establish, the more effective your efforts will be.

When asking your questions, practice good interviewing techniques. For example, you should listen carefully! If you don't, you might ask a question that you just got the answer to. You should also use the decision maker's name frequently. Finally, don't be afraid of pauses. Silent periods between questions can be helpful to you both. And remember that if you do a good job the first time, you will have an opportunity to come back a second time— perhaps you will be coming back for the rest of your working life. This will give you plenty of time to get all the answers you need.

While the decision maker is speaking, watch and listen. How is this person reacting to you? Concentrate on the positives—the things that work well and seem to bring a good response.

You should also try to identify with this person. On the basis of the decision maker's answers to your questions, speaking ability, and so on, try to determine his or her socioeconomic background. Verbal skills and abilities tell a great deal about a person.

If the decision maker came up from the bottom, the hard way, you will probably learn about this during the interview. Try to identify with such a background. If you have done some of the same things—worked your way through college, for example— you might mention this. You can also identify with the decision maker by noticing such things as pictures and trophies in the office. Things like this are good clues to a person's "hot buttons."

What you'll be looking for

You should question the decision maker in a way that will allow you to identify and define:
1. His or her opportunities (challenges)
2. His or her needs and wants (desires)
3. What it will take to satisfy these

Basically, you will be concerned with the following questions in trying to determine the decision maker's "hot buttons":
1. What does he or she want?
2. What should I offer?
3. What benefits are attractive to this person?
4. What should I communicate so that he or she will buy?

Obviously, you can't ask the above questions specifically. This would show no tact and would be self-defeating. Remember that you are seeking information and are bargaining from a position of strength.

The decision maker will provide you with a wealth of information if you do your job as a listener. Many of your questions about money, growth, opportunities, problems, successes, etc., will be answered without your having to ask. Decision makers will tell you about mistakes made by others and about their own successes and accomplishments—*if* they want you to know. But don't push for such information the first time around. The more decision makers talk, the more they want to talk. Remember that they are helping themselves as well as you by concentrating on the reasons for their success.

Questions to ask during the interview

The questions you ask during the consulting interview must be general ones. Specific questions concerning a certain salary, etc., are to be reserved for the formal interview situation. This is only common courtesy. You don't want to ask questions that will put the decision maker on the defensive. You want the decision maker to talk with you about himself or herself. By asking specific questions, you might create distances between the two of you instead of building bridges.

Remember that the questions listed below are only examples. They're meant to help you formulate your own questions. Try changing them around to suit your own style and your own thinking and personality.

All your questions could well be contained in the first three. The rest of the questions are meant to help you direct the interview and bring it back in line if the decision maker should stray too far.

1. How did you get to this point in your career?
2. Would you have done it any other way?
3. Are you glad that you're here?
4. What word would you use to describe the personality of this company and this industry?
5. What do you feel is the future of this industry?
6. What do you feel is the future of your company in this industry?
7. Why did you choose this industry and this company?
8. What facet of this industry or related industries has the greatest growth potential? Which has the greatest profit potential?
9. Why is your product (or service) different from that of your competition?
10. How long have you been in this industry and with this company?
11. Which companies in this industry have the best training programs, initial and ongoing? Why do you feel that way?
12. Who are some of the other top people in the company?
13. How did they come up the ladder?
14. What are the goals and philosophies of your company?
15. Could you give me the names of at least two other exceptional executives in this industry whom I might approach in the same manner I've approached you?
16. Are there any questions I should have asked that I didn't?

Questions concerning corporate structure, income levels, company problems, etc., *must* wait until the formal, or follow-up, interview. Again, if the decision maker wants you to know about some of these matters, he or she will volunteer the information.

Use some discretion

Don't put all your cards on the table, even if a potential employer comes right out and asks you whether you are looking for a job. An honest reply is called for in this case, however:

"Well, I'm not sure. Quite frankly, I'm not on the job market now. I might be soon because of this conversation and others, but then again I might find out that "the grass really isn't greener." But you might help me to discover those important secrets to success that I've been missing, and maybe I'll be able to help you as well."

On the positive side, when a decision maker asks whether you are looking for a job, this can provide you with an additional entrée, either by phone or, preferably, through the use of the personal profile. For example:

"When we met a couple of weeks ago, you asked whether I was looking for a job. I've done a lot of thinking, and in answer to your question, I'm not looking for a job. I'm looking for an opportunity to contribute and grow professionally. I'd like to meet with you again and discuss some of my potential and ideas in this regard."

or

"I was quite impressed during and after our meeting. Since that time, I've spoken with eight or ten other executives. I think we hit it off quite well, and now I'd like to meet with you to discuss how I might contribute to your company's continuing growth and successes."

But now we're getting ahead of ourselves. Let's return to the interview.

The conclusion

Questions such as those listed above will make the decision maker interested in you. He or she will be interested because your questions reflect your attitude and your concern and show that you're obviously well prepared. By giving you the answers to your questions, the decision maker is showing this interest. Drop it right there. No hard push or hard sell is called for here.

The decision maker might well close the meeting by saying, "Well, let's get together and talk about you sometime." You could reply:

"Fine, I'd like to do that. There are a lot of things I'd like to go over with you. Thanks for your time, your counsel, and your advice."

Believe me, the decision maker will remember who *you* are. When you next approach this person for an interview (or vice versa), it will be an entirely different story.

Information the decision maker
will want about you

The decision maker might say, "We've talked a lot about me; now I'd like to know something about you as well." In this case, play it down. Talk about yourself, but keep it brief. For example:

> "I'm with the ABC Corporation, where I'm Assistant Vice President of their _____ department. At this point, I'm kind of frustrated—possibly I'm too ambitious or impatient. I'm married, and have a couple of kids. I'm at a crossroads; I'm just not certain which road to take. That's pretty much who I am in a nutshell. Now, all your good ideas have given me a lot to think about."

or

> "As I said when we first spoke, I'm at a crossroads. I'm up for a promotion. If I don't accept it—corporate death. If I do, there's a good possibility it'll end up being more of the same. I just don't know, nor am I asking you to make the decision for me. I'm going home to do a lot of thinking for the next couple of days. I'll be in touch, and thanks again."

Yes, reveal a little about yourself. Then get back to having your questions answered. If the interview is finished and the decision maker still wants to talk—great. Be a good sounding board. Remember, the more information you can glean, the more material, ideas, and insights you'll have to work with and the easier it will be for you to make an intelligent and informed decision.

"How about sending me your
résumé?"

A decision maker who asks this is interested in moving further with you. You might answer:

> "Sure, I'll have something in the mail for you in the next couple of days."

or

> "Well, as I said, I'm not presently on the job market, so I don't have a current résumé. I'll be happy to send you something in the mail as soon as I put it together, OK?"

If you've asked for half an hour and you've gotten an hour, that's more than enough. Don't push a good thing.

Immediately after the consulting interview

Immediately following an interview, it's imperative that you find a nice quiet place where you can sort out your thoughts and feelings about the industry, the company, and the decision maker as a person and a professional.

You should have a score sheet on which to write down any additional thoughts or ideas that weren't covered during the interview. Don't trust this information to memory. Write it down to clarify it and fix it in your mind. Because you'll be conducting between fifteen and twenty-five informal meetings, it's important that you remember "who was who."

CONSULTING INTERVIEW DEBRIEFING SCORE SHEET

PERSONAL INFORMATION ABOUT THE DECISION MAKER
Name:
Company: Unique characteristics:
Approximate age:
Attitude:
Physical appearance:

PROFESSIONAL INFORMATION ABOUT THE DECISION MAKER
First impressions:

Decision maker's "hot buttons":   Pet peeves:

Personality type:

Do you identify with, and relate to, this person?

Could you work with this person? Why?

Do you like this person? Why? Do you dislike anything about this person?

Did this person give you a good overview of the company? If not, what could you have done or what will you do to correct this?

Which questions weren't answered during the interview? Were they important? Why?

Were there any questions you discovered in addition to these that really worked well? What were they?

Should you rearrange these questions so they'll flow more easily? What other questions did you ask or should you have asked?

Could you have done something to make the interview move more quickly or flow more easily? What was it?

What successes did you achieve? How can you capitalize on these?

Did you make any mistakes? What were they? How will you avoid these in the future?

What was your reaction to this situation? Are you ready to go further?

Could you really do an outstanding job for this person? Why?

What are the chances that you can fully utilize your skills with this person?

What was some of the information confided in you about the company? About the industry?

What are some of this person's major accomplishments and secrets to success?

Does this person behave in a professional manner?

What is the corporate personality?

Is this compatible with your personality? Why?

Miscellaneous:

Follow-up

As soon as you get home, write a thank-you letter. This is important:
1. It shows your ability to follow up.
2. It shows your good manners, courtesy, and consideration.
3. It reinforces your thanks to the person you received a favor from.
4. It cements your contact with this person.

Of course, you'll want to give special attention to some of these people. With them, you might follow up with something similar to the personal profile, discussed in detail in the following chapter (see also Appendix A).

One final thought

I can't help but recall a quotation here regarding the importance of gaining as much exposure as possible, interviewing as much as possible, and finding out what the world has to offer. That quotation, from the show *Auntie Mame,* is as follows: "Life's a banquet and most poor bastards are starving to death."

NINE

The Professional Profile

Now that you've been through some informal consulting interviews, do you feel you need any more practice? If you don't, then it's on to the real thing. You've made your mistakes, and you'll probably make some more, but let's concentrate on what you have done right. You're already way ahead of everyone else, and so now it's onward and upward.

If you've done your homework and handled your consulting interviews in an intelligent and knowledgeable manner, then you will have gained some knowledge of each decision maker's:

1. Problems (opportunities and challenges)
2. Needs and wants
3. Desires

Now it's up to you to determine what it will take to satisfy these needs and solve these problems and to decide whether you've got what it takes to do this. If you think you do, the next step is to methodically develop the product that each decision maker requires. This will require that you systematically go over the results of your exercises and pick out those skills, talents, abilities, attitudes, goals, characteristics, etc., which pertain to the individual decision maker's problems, needs, and desires.

After the interview

How often, after an interview, have you wished you had had at least another hour (maybe more) with the interviewer? There were so many things that you didn't have time to say. Here's where good common sense comes in again. You should follow up on this feeling, but not in a haphazard manner. Now is the time to take action—to show those carefully selected decision makers your uniqueness and potential. Now is the time to carefully place yourself in contention for that niche.

How do you do this? By taking all your knowledge, experience, and potential and putting them together in a truly professional, appealing, intelligent, and customized presentation. In essence, you will be telling these people what they need, but in such a professional and enticing manner that they can't help but seriously consider you for a possible position.

You are about to show these decision makers not only how you can save them time, effort, and money but also how you can contribute substantially to the evolution and development of these commodities within their companies. Let's take these benefits one at a time:

1. You can help them save money by hiring you directly, thus avoiding search or employment agency fees, the cost of newspaper ads, and so on.
2. You can help them make this experience a pleasant one, not a chore. Point this out by appealing to each decision maker from all angles—mention the pleasant consulting interview and other encounters yet to come, for example.
3. You can help them save time and effort by avoiding the communications problems connected with a search or recruiting effort, as well as the interviewing problems and other negatives discussed in earlier chapters.

The professional profile defined

The professional profile is a vivid and concise outline of you as a professional contributor. This customized[1] presentation tells who you are: what you can do best and where you feel you can

---

[1] Each profile must be individually prepared to appeal specifically to a particular company, industry, and decision maker. For example, you should include in your profile a number of individualized comments which the particular decision maker will agree with and identify with. The decision maker will then be a willing and responsive reader of your efforts. Your profile must be designed so that the person who reads it will relate to it directly and personally.

contribute to the company's growth, development, and ongoing success.

Anyone can talk, but writing a presentation takes a lot of time and effort. It will be appreciated more than any résumé or anything presented by a third party. It is meaningful, and it hits home.

Psychologists' profiles

Recognizing the need for such a profile, industry long ago enlisted psychologists to create:
1. The professional evaluation report
2. The personality profile
3. The candidate profile

Yes, these do have merit, but psychologists will be the first to admit that you know yourself better than anyone else ever will. After doing the exercises in Chapter 3, you have a very good understanding of your strengths, weaknesses, skills, philosophies, goals, and aspirations. Aren't these more meaningful than the items on a psychologist's profile? For example:
1. Supervisory index
2. Intellectual capacity
3. Verbal comprehension
4. Space visualization
5. Numerical reasoning

Psychologists' profiles have a place and a value, but what could be more important than your own commonsense, honest self-appraisal?

The contents of your profile

Look at the profile in Appendix A. As you can see, it includes the following:
1. An introduction
2. An honest enumeration of your general and specific skills and abilities
3. A listing of your own professional goals and aspirations
4. A rundown of your pertinent experience and credentials (relating directly to your chosen industry and to this specific company)
5. Your credo and professional philosophies
6. Pertinent personal specifics with disclaimer
7. Supporting documentation
8. A proper closing

A two-edged sword

The professional profile has many advantages, but it can be a two-edged sword.

Edge one

If you honestly discuss yourself and your abilities, you can carve the right position in the right company and in the right industry. Why? Because you are creating the position as you and you alone can do it. There is no one in the world who can do the job as you can because you have built this position for your own unique personality and professional abilities. This is a position which only you can monopolize and exploit.

Edge two

If you are not honest in your appraisal of yourself, you will be carving a false niche, and this will become all too apparent, and within a very short period of time. Then what have you achieved?

Goals of the professional profile

As you compose your profile, remember that its purposes are:
1. To provide each potential employer with a unique and customized appraisal of you and your capabilities
2. To assist you in thinking of yourself as a special and unique asset to a potential group of employers
3. To present you in an appealing, persuasive, and common-sense way
4. To assist you in carving that niche for yourself

A word of caution

Of course, this is only one approach. If you can come up with a better one, more power to you. Be sure to assess carefully whether your own approach is tasteful, professional, and truly representative of you. It must be honest and provide you with direct access to the decision makers.

In my research, I've come across many creative approaches to presenting oneself, getting attention, etc. However, most of these sacrifice professionalism for effect, which is definitely not what you want.

Putting a profile together

A profile is not put together in a few minutes or hours. It requires a lot of work and introspection, and it takes many hours, perhaps days, of writing and rewriting. It must flow logically and have fire—fire to motivate the person who will read it to seriously consider you for a definite position with the company.

The professional profile is a kind of biography of your professional life. Thus it is not something to be taken lightly or to be done by anyone else. This is a "one-of-a-kind" presentation of you and by you.

Hints on preparation

1. Go back to the exercises you did in Chapter 3. This is where you'll really make use of your efforts to identify your unique skills, abilities, philosophies, and experience. This is where you can provide each decision maker with persuasive insights into your makeup, personality, and potential to contribute.

2. Review the notes you made prior to the consulting interview. Then go over the notes you made at the end of the consulting interview for additional ammunition, insights, and ideas. This will enable you to deal directly with the decision maker's problems and needs.

3. Label five sheets of paper as follows:

   a. Philosophies and personal credo
   b. Skills, talents, and abilities
   c. Goals
   d. Experience, including major contributions
   e. Each decision maker's "hot buttons"

Then start writing, organizing, and rewriting.

4. Put your thoughts down on paper in paragraph form and in longhand. Once you feel you have covered the basics, have this typed. Now cut the paragraphs apart and reassemble them in a different order. Strive for continuity of thought as well as readability. Do you repeat yourself? Unless you do this for effect, get rid of the repetition. Once you have pieced the entire presentation together, make an outline. Does it flow? Is it logical? Then have your presentation retyped.

5. Have you included negatives? Yes, this *is* a totally positive experience, but no one is perfect. Remember that you are making an honest self-appraisal and that you have some negative facets in you makeup. Include them, but be sure to show how they can

be beneficial as well. For example, you might say, "Although I am not a college graduate, I look upon this as an asset. I have accepted this as part of my makeup and realize that I have to work, in some cases twice as hard, to make sure that I always come out ahead of the college grads." You could also say something like, "I'm overly conscientious. I get too involved in my work for my own good and that of my family. I'm a workaholic." Don't discuss periods of unemployment. This subject will be dealt with during the formal interview, not the consulting interview.

6. Show your profile to your husband or wife or to a friend whose opinions you respect. Ask for constructive criticism. This will provide you with other insights into who you really are and will help you understand what you're projecting to someone else. Ask this person to be highly critical. That's exactly what your potential employer is going to be.

7. Avoid using the word "I" as much as possible. Watch for spelling and punctuation errors. These can be disastrous.

8. Put the profile away for at least a day, longer if possible. Then read it again very carefully and critically. Make any final changes and have it typed again.

An outside opinion

It is important to get one or more additional outside opinions. This will also give you some extra exposure. Take your profile to some business people whose opinions you respect. Explain what you're doing and say that you'd like their constructive criticism. Ask them to look your profile over carefully, at their leisure, and to make any notes and comments right on the profile.

Packaging

Many copy centers and printshops provide a service called Velo-Bind. This permanent binding looks impressive and is not too expensive. Your presentation is very important and serious, and its appearance should reflect this.

I can't overemphasize the importance of making your profile as attractive, inviting, and commanding of each decision maker's attention as possible. The cover must reflect its quality and the effort you've expended on its preparation. You might include a tasteful picture of yourself (don't make it a full-page one) to jog the decision maker's memory. You might also include pictures of projects you've worked on. Graphs can also help to tell your story. In short, use your imagination and your good taste.

Don't worry if each profile costs $2, $5, or even $10. It will be money well spent—invested in your future. Your profile will be something the decision makers won't dismiss, deposit in the circular file, or put off until tomorrow.

When you've finished your packaging, pat yourself on the back for the fine job you've done. Then put your profiles in the mail.

Timing and your profile

Within about a week after you've mailed your personalized profiles (don't send more than five or so), you will start to receive phone calls or letters arranging for a *formal* follow-up interview. Remember to give the decision makers time to review your profile carefully. In dealing from a position of strength, you mustn't be overly anxious.

Be sure to space the interviews at least two or more days apart. (Take large helpings of stress vitamins well in advance.)

Do not bring your profile to the interview

Your profile is an in-depth self-appraisal, and you'll want each decision maker to give it some time and review it completely. *This simply cannot be done when you're sitting right there.* It just won't work. This is the kind of thing the decision maker will want to take home or review carefully on a quiet Friday afternoon.

Preparation for the follow-up interview

Now that you've submitted your professional profile, the next important step is *your* final preparation.

1. Are you ready to ask and answer questions intelligently and knowledgeably?
2. Have you completed your homework on the company? Have you done all your research?
3. Have you checked out the areas in which you discovered you had weaknesses? Did you strengthen them?
4. Have you emphasized the things that worked?

5. Have you studied the materials you got during each consulting interview?
6. Which questions didn't you get answers to at each consulting interview? Should you include these in the follow-up interview?

In the next chapter we'll be discussing techniques of formal interviewing that have been proved effective—that work!

A final caution

Don't proceed any further unless:
1. You have your listing of:
   a. Five (specific) contributions you made to your former (or present) employer
   b. Five areas in which you can make contributions to each chosen company
   c. Five reasons why you specifically want a position with each selected company
2. You have done all the necessary informal interviewing
3. You are confident of your ability to handle just about anything the various interviewers can throw at you
4. You have sent out your profiles to each of the companies which you've identified as offering you the greatest chance for professional growth and ongoing career development

TEN

Test Marketing: Techniques of Formal Interviewing[1]

After you've done your research (determined needs, wants, and desires), and developed your basic product (your professional profile), you will follow up by going back (when invited) to these same decision makers or to people to whom they have referred you.

You may have found during your consulting interviews that you're "right" for one of several companies. The follow-up interview will help you to decide which company is right for you.

Your test marketing is done through additional interviewing, but interviewing of a *formal* nature. During your follow-up interviews you're continually doing marketing research and trying to develop your knowledge and understanding, carefully and methodically. You're striving to show how you can perform in your identified niche.

This chapter suggests a method or technique for formal interviewing activities. You might well go into an interview and find that the interviewer has never read this book (or any others on the subject), and perhaps doesn't know the first thing about how to

[1]I've entitled this chapter "test marketing" because this "sale" will continue for as long as you stay with your chosen employer.

conduct an interview properly. If that's the case, you'll have to take the reins, but again, *be yourself—no matter what.* This chapter will provide you with the fundamental principles of interviewing. Do your best to cover these basics and, most important, remember that it's always better to be overprepared than underprepared.

Your enthusiastic attitude means everything

Your enthusiastic belief in yourself and in your future is what it's all about. All you can do is to try. If you fail, maybe this company just isn't for you, and it's on to the next one—on to newer and greater challenges, opportunities, and endeavors. I'm certain you realize that you're much further ahead because of the experience and knowledge you've gained as you've read this book and done the exercises. You're certainly further ahead than if you had spent this time writing résumés that couldn't really have told your story.

Selling yourself

Perhaps one of the most entertaining things in the world today is seeing a good salesperson in action (there are so few good ones)—someone who has done his or her homework and research, who knows the product's assets as well as its liabilities, and who understands how to make the best of both of these.

In selling yourself, it's important for you to concentrate on important matters and to rid yourself of all unnecessary concerns (Chapters 1 and 2), to know yourself (Chapter 3), to know your target (Chapter 4), to be prepared (Chapter 5), and to set the stage and get the practice to make sure that everything will go smoothly for the sale (Chapters 6 to 9). This is an exciting adventure—your hunt for success.

"Professionals" defined

Some of my feelings regarding the makeup of true professionals include the following. Professionals are people who:

Have recognized their strengths and their weaknesses.

Take an active role in determining their future and what's going to happen to them. That is, they continually strive to maximize their career opportunities.

Are dignified and in harmony with their surroundings.

Make decisions and accept the fact that they will be making mistakes as well as achieving successes.

Are honest with themselves and with those around them.

Have established realistic personal and professional goals and continually strive to achieve them.

Have savvy.

Have the ability to evaluate others. They don't play God or feel sorry for others.

Are humble.

Know themselves.

Don't feel guilty when they have to say "no."

Recognize that their strengths are found in their ability to deal with others as people.

Do their job to the best of their ability and gain confidence from having accomplished something in a first-class manner.

Have the ability to listen to others and evaluate their needs.

Have learned to gain assistance from others—without having to demand it.

Don't spread themselves too thin.

Are "doers."

Inspire confidence.

When that decision is made

All professionals reach a point where they get ready to graduate to the big time, the big dollars, and the big opportunities. Perhaps this occurs when they are no longer satisfied playing the day-in, day-out numbers game, when they recognize that they will have to take the initiative if they are ever going to move ahead and become successful, or when they learn to accept responsibility —for both their successes and their failures. Perhaps this point is reached when a person says, "I refuse to trust my future and my potential in life to others," "I'm tired of just doing a job," or "I'm drowning in a sea of mediocrity, and all these people are making it big; just think of what I could do if—" and then does something about it. Or, finally, this point might be reached when a person realizes that there will *always* be room at the top for a true professional.

This is the hard time, when those who have intestinal fortitude commit themselves to their professional growth, really do the job (as it should be done), keep their sights on that faraway goal of success, and *make* that goal come closer. That's when the true pro carefully identifies problems; works *with* people to determine their "hot buttons," their needs, and their desires; and then methodically equates their needs to his or her product or service and its benefits and to the way this product can solve their problems.

Your interviewing sales goal

Your first goal is to help each interviewer[2] identify what he or she truly needs and wants. (Remember that wants and needs can be considerably different.) Then you must show how your unique talents and abilities will satisfy these needs and wants; you must project yourself into a mutually identified position so that you can help the interviewer "buy" you.

The happiest "buyers" will tell you that their boss, employer, manager, wife, or husband (the "seller"):

1. Listens when they talk about their needs and works to satisfy them
2. Talks *with* them, not *to* them
3. Identifies what can be accomplished if they do something (helps them to buy benefits, not products)
4. Helps them to do things—to achieve goals (helps them buy)
5. Treats them the way they'd like to be treated

For example, what do you think your chances will be if you say to a potential employer, "How about a job? In the past, I've made $20,000 a year, but I'm willing to accept just about anything"? Although this might be a slight exaggeration, that's just about the way most people go about trying to get a job.

The rest of this chapter will be devoted to telling you how to handle the formal interview situation—the proved way, the right way. We'll concentrate on selling the benefits you can provide if you're hired. In short, don't sell yourself or your abilities. Help your prospective employer to buy the benefits that you, your skills, talents, and abilities can provide.

In review

1. Find a company with problems that you can solve.
2. Help the decision maker identify the problems and the potential benefits if they were solved.

---

[2]Your formal interview might well be with an executive other than the decision maker. This is done for the purpose of confirming or denying the latter's impression of you.

3. Talk in terms of the decision maker's own interests, not yours.
4. Tell your story with warmth, sincerity, enthusiasm, and conviction.
5. Outline for the decision maker what can be achieved if you come on board.

Remember that all-important commandment concerned with the decision maker. Real pros will meet and deal almost exclusively with the decision maker. They concentrate their efforts, in a persistent and determined manner, on demonstrating to that person the benefits that their product or service will provide for the company.

Why is someone hired?

Here are some of the most common reasons a person is hired:

1. The person can make and/or save money for the company (the single most important reason—contributing to the bottom line).
2. The decision maker likes and identifies with the person.
3. The person can satisfy a need (i.e., can identify, define, and solve problems).
4. He or she is there and is bright and willing.
5. There was a need for someone.
6. The person wants and asks for the position and *has valid reasons for doing so.*
7. The person can do something the decision maker doesn't have the time or ability to do.
8. He or she can do the job better and more reasonably than anyone else.
9. The decision maker can handle the person (the person is not threatening to the decision maker).
10. The person has been referred by a friend of the decision maker.
11. The person has the qualifications, knowledge, experience, etc., which the decision maker thinks are necessary to handle the position.

Definitions for review

Business

A business can be defined as an entity created to solve problems and to make a profit while doing this.

Problem

A problem is an opportunity (challenge) looking for a solution. For example, your problem is that you need something to sit on. You go to a store and purchase a chair. The store sells you the chair, thus solving your problem and (it hopes) making a profit. This is a simplistic example, but it contains all the basics.

Now let's take your present situation. If you're changing companies within a specific industry or moving to a closely related one, the interviewers you meet with might talk about some of their problems. They're searching for answers—that's part of their job. By alluding to your ability to handle these problems—such as by giving examples of how you effectively handled similar ones while with your former employer—you are telling the interviewers what they *need* to hear.

Caution: You may be treading on very thin ice here. If you're undergoing a career change or an industry change, *don't presume to know the answers to all their problems.* And remember that it's not only what you've done that's important—it's what you *can* do!

Interviewing

Interviewing is the process of selecting the candidate, from a pool of potential candidates, who has the greatest potential to contribute to the growth and success of a company.

Selection

Selection is prediction. A decision maker who selects you to do a job for his or her organization is predicting that you will succeed in that position.

Initial interview

The initial interview (also known as the screening interview or preliminary interview) is a short interview session held to screen out all but the most likely candidates.

Selection interview

A selection interview is an intensive meeting between a candidate and a company representative for the purpose of gaining information about the candidate and allowing for the selection of the most desirable candidate for a position.

Follow-up interview

A follow-up interview is a meeting between a candidate and a selected interviewer which allows both parties to acquire in-depth information prior to a possible hiring.

Hiring interview

A hiring interview is a meeting between the decision maker and the chosen candidate during which final understandings are reached prior to the person's being hired.[3]

Preparation for the follow-up interview

First you must review where you are. Go over the notes you took during and after the consulting interview and cover every possible problem, challenge, and opportunity you encountered. Concentrate on the positives—the things that worked best and were most appealing to the decision makers. Be aware of the negatives.

Goals of the formal interview

The whole goal of preparing yourself for the follow-up interview is to help you "hire yourself an employer"[4] by calling the employer's attention to:
1. Your personal and professional accomplishments
2. Your unique skills, abilities, and potential to contribute
3. Those matters not covered on your profile

An important word of caution

Do not lie at an interview. If you do, here are some of the things that can happen (and probably will):
1. You might get the job, but suddenly both you and your employer will find that:
   a. You're unable to do the job you said you could.
   b. You're unhappy, and the company is unhappy.
   c. Your references won't stand up.
2. You won't get the job because, in checking, it becomes apparent that you've misrepresented yourself, which is cause for immediate termination anyway. Remember that it's a small world; word gets around fast and former employers, etc., don't want to be associated with a liar.
3. You'll make many people look bad:
   a. Yourself

[3]The follow-up interview and the hiring interview are the only formal ones which should be of concern to you in using the methods proposed in this book. Be advised that all the interviews discussed here can be combined into one session or stretched out into many sessions over an extended period of time.

[4]The title of a book by Richard Irish on the subject of job hunting.

b. The person who hired you

c. The other parties to the hiring

d. The people who were counting on you to do the job

The application form

If you are given an application form, either before or after the interview, ask permission to take it with you and fill it out at home. Remember that you're there to be interviewed, not to fill out forms—and how can you fill them out anyway when the information you need is at home?

If you must fill out a form, you should do it right. I'll go into a considerable amount of detail regarding the application form in the next chapter.

The formal interview: a broad overview

Like the informal consulting interview, the formal interview consists of three basic parts:

1. The introduction (to include purpose)
2. The body (the selling and buying section), which is composed of:
   a. The company's sell
   b. Questions and answers (yours and theirs)
   c. The candidate's sell
3. The closing
   Let's discuss each of these in detail.

The introduction

Don't be overly friendly with the secretary—you're still a stranger. Once you are in the inner sanctum, be professionally warm and sincere. As in the consulting interview, after the social amenities have been dispensed with, you must take control, both of yourself and of the interview.

If you aren't yet on a first-name basis with the decision maker, wait until he or she calls you by your first name; that's your signal to do the same.[5]

Remember that this is a totally positive experience. Your

[5]Be advised that the formal interview may be with the decision maker, the person who will be your immediate superior, or any one of a number of other people in the company.

purpose is to help yourself and to help others. No negatives allowed! You're going to buy the company and the position and *sell* yourself. The interviewer is going to *sell* his or her company and buy you and your services—your potential. Remember to be enthusiastic, right from the moment you meet each interviewer.

The body

The interviewer may well start the meeting by saying something like, "Tell me about yourself." Interviewers do this because very few of them have ever been taught the fundamentals of interviewing. Thus you may have to do some subtle "instructing" of your own. You might answer this as follows:

"Well, I'm a_____ year-old who's done a lot of research on your company and this industry. I have some questions to ask you. I'm very impressed with your record of growth, your imaginative products, and the position you've achieved in this industry."

or

"I'm very impressed with the imaginative _____ you've been marketing. That's the reason I'm here. And I'm very anxious to ask you a number of questions. May I?"

or

"I have a number of questions I'd like to ask you right off, so if you don't mind, could we postpone me for awhile?"

or

"I know you have a lot of questions to ask me, but before we start that, I've got some that I really need the answers to. Mostly they're concerned with the reasons why you like this company."[6]

The right questions

When researching needs and problems associated with any industry, company, or product, you'll be concerned in some way with those questions we outlined earlier:

1. What does the company want?
2. What employee characteristics are attractive to it?
3. What should I be able to do for the company?

[6]Knowledgeable interviewers will be prepared to tell you about the reasons for their success with the company, why they like it, and their major areas of contribution. This is an integral part of their sales pitch.

4. What should I communicate about myself?

You will be able to come up with many different ways of phrasing these questions, but here are a few examples:

Do you have a specific position in mind?[7]

What are you looking for in the person who will fill this position?

Where might I fit into your organization?

Could you tell me something about the duties and responsibilities of such a position?

What are the pertinent things you'd like to know about my background and experience and their relevance to this position?

In what kind of position do you feel I could make the greatest contributions to this company? Why?

What objectives would you like to see achieved by the person holding such a position?

What kind of background, knowledge, and experience would best qualify a person to achieve such objectives in the shortest period of time?

Try to ask as many questions as soon as possible after the interview begins. Why? Because *if you listen carefully, you will find that the interviewer will tell you exactly what he or she wants to hear.* The things the interviewer emphasizes are the things that he or she wants to hear about you—your past, your background, and your experience, as well as your unique potential and ability to contribute. As in the consulting interview, write each of these key points down and be sure to go over them. Tell the interviewer what he or she wants to hear. I've restated this so many times because it is important. This is the interviewer's *sell* section of the interview.

Remember to listen very carefully to what the decision maker (interviewer) is saying. Don't be thinking about what you are going to say. If you listen, you will be arming yourself with the knowledge that will propel you into your niche.

Also remember to take notes while the interviewer is talking. The interview is a stress situation. You can't possibly be expected to remember each point. Furthermore, taking notes is very professional and shows both your organizational ability and your interest in the position. Only when the interviewer is *finished*

---

[7]It's only fair that the interviewer tell you about the specific position so that you'll both be talking about the same thing.

with the sell should you start your sales pitch. The interviewer will lead the way for you with questions.

Remember that your attitude is everything. It should be positive and enthusiastic. Enthusiasm is tremendously contagious. Unless you're enthusiastic about yourself and your potential to contribute to the company, how can you expect the interviewer to be enthusiastic about you?

After answering your first few questions, the interviewer should have told you about the company and sold you on its opportunities. But it's also at this point that the interviewer might well start asking you some very important and pointed questions—stress questions.

I strongly suggest that you take a pencil and some paper and answer the following stress questions in detail. After a few days, review your answers until you (your toughest critic) are satisfied with them. Be sure to file the answers to these questions in your success manual for your ongoing updating and review during your interviewing efforts.

Questions about the industry of your choosing

1. What is your overall impression of this industry?
2. What kind of research have you done regarding this industry?
3. Who are some of the people you've spoken with in this industry?
4. Why have you chosen this industry?
5. Where, in your estimation, is this industry's greatest growth potential? Why? Where is this industry weakest? Why?
6. How do you view the short-term future of this industry? Why? How do you view its long-term future? Why?
7. What major problems do you anticipate this industry will face in the future?
8. What do you view as this industry's greatest problem or problems?
9. Do you have any ideas or suggestions concerning the solutions to these problems?
10. What other industries are you considering? Why?
11. Do you have any dislikes or reservations regarding this industry? What are they? Why do you feel this way?
12. How do you view competition in this industry?

13. What do you consider to be the most important skill necessary to achieve success in this industry?

Questions about the company of your choosing

1. What do you know about our company?
2. What would you like to know about our company?
3. Why would you like to go to work for our company?
4. What kind of recommendations could we expect from your former employer?
5. Why are you leaving your present employer?
6. How long would you plan to stay with us?
7. Where do you feel you might be able to contribute to our company?
8. How long do you feel it would take you to make a contribution to our company? Why?
9. In your present position, what problems have you identified that had been previously overlooked?
10. What did you do to effect their solution?
11. Don't you feel you might be better off in a smaller company or a different type of company? Wouldn't you be happier in a company with a more tangible product?
12. What do you think of your present manager?
13. What kind of research have you done regarding our company?
14. Have there been any long periods of unemployment in your work history? What were the circumstances regarding these periods?
15. Would you draw me the organization chart of your present employer and show where you fit in?
16. What criteria do you use to evaluate a company you wish to work for?
17. Is company size important to you? Why?
18. Why do you think you'd like to live in this community?
19. In which areas do you feel you can contribute to the growth and ongoing success of this company?
20. What do you think it takes to be successful in a company like ours?

Questions about the position of your choosing

1. What position in our company will you be striving for? Why?
2. In which position do you feel you could make the greatest

contributions to our company? Why?

3. What interests you most about our product?

4. What do you regard as some of the most important lessons you have learned from the positions you've held? Why?

5. Which features of your previous positions have you liked? Why? Which ones have you disliked? Why?

6. Describe some situations in which your efforts have been praised. Why were they praised? Describe some situations in which you were criticized. Why were you criticized?

7. What do you consider to be the most important contributions you have made to your present employer? Why?

8. Name five unique contributions you can make to our company that someone else can't.

9. What do you consider to be your greatest potential area for contributing to our company? Why do you feel you can contribute in this area?

10. Why did you accept each of the positions listed on your résumé?

11. In these positions, describe your salary increases. Were they offered, or did you have to ask for them?

12. How many people did you supervise in your last position? Did you feel that you could handle that many effectively?

13. We have three positions open in our company. After I describe each one, would you tell me which you'd prefer and why?

14. How large a budget have you been responsible for?

15. Have you ever fired anyone? Why did you do this? How did you do this?

16. Have you ever put your position on the line for something you strongly believed in? Tell me about this.

17. Which is more important to you, money or position?

18. What kind of relationship should exist between managers and those reporting to them?

19. What qualities and personal characteristics must a successful manager have? Why?

20. What is your definition of the "ideal position"?

21. Quite frankly, why should I hire you?

22. What are the highest skill levels (relating to people, data, and things) at which you feel confident of functioning? Can you tell me why you feel this way and give me some examples of your effective use of these skills?

23. How much emphasis do you place on staying with the

basics? Do you work at this continually? Can you give me some examples of how you concern yourself with these?

24. Aren't you overqualified for this position?

Questions about your personal and professional life

1. What do you consider to be your greatest strengths? Why?
2. What do you consider to be your greatest weaknesses? Why?
3. What are your short-term goals? Your intermediate-term goals? Your long-term goals?
4. When and why did you establish these goals?
5. What are some of the new goals you have recently established?
6. How do you plan to accomplish these goals?
7. What are your most important considerations and concerns in seeking a position?
8. What do you consider to be your greatest accomplishments?
9. What does the word "success" mean to you?
10. If you could start all over again, what would you do differently? Why?
11. What kind of income are you worth? Why?
12. Do you have good leadership capabilities? What are some examples of your success as a leader?
13. Could you tell me five unique features of your personality which you feel contribute to your success?
14. Could you give me some examples of your creative skills and abilities?
15. Are you detail-oriented? Can you give me a few examples?
16. Would you be a good manager? Why?
17. What are some of your philosophies regarding _____ [sales and marketing, for example]?
18. What is your reaction to pressure? To crisis thinking? To deadlines?
19. What makes you different from other _____ [salesmen, managers, executives, etc.]? Why do you say this?
20. What does the term "cooperation" mean to you?
21. Does your family take an active interest in your professional life?
22. What does the word "initiative" mean to you? Could you tell me about some times you have used initiative in your professional life?

23. What do you think are the best parameters to use in pegging a person's progress in a company?
24. How would you and your family feel about relocating to this area?
25. Do you have a geographic preference?
26. How would you and your family feel about your traveling 10 percent of the time?
27. Could you tell me something about your interests and your hobbies?
28. What is your financial position? Do you have any serious financial problems?
29. Which magazines and books have you read recently? Do you read industry-related publications frequently?
30. Have you taken college courses to enhance your knowledge and understanding of this industry?
31. Have you taken advantage of industry-related training programs? Have you found these to be helpful?
32. How do you feel about continuing education?
33. Why do you feel qualified for this particular position?
34. What do you *really* want to do with your life?
35. How would you describe yourself?
36. How would a close friend describe you? A business associate?
37. What motivates you to put forth your best efforts?
38. Tell me about a big mistake you've made. What did you learn from this?
39. Can you give me an example of a major problem you ran into and tell me how you solved it?
40. What do you expect to be earning next year? In five years? In ten years? Why?
41. Why did you choose this career field?
42. What are some of the qualifications you possess which make you think you'll be successful in this business?
43. Do you use drugs? Do you drink excessively?
44. You've been telling me that you increased sales and profits substantially with your former employer. Could you tell me exactly how you accomplished this?

Answering stress questions

As you can see, a lot of thinking and preparation are necessary in order to answer stress questions well. However, don't try to memorize answers to questions like those listed above. Stress questions are meant to enable the interviewer to know you better.

When the interviewer replies "Why?" to one of your answers, your response must be honest and off the cuff.

Develop that sixth sense, the one concerned with integrity. Do you feel comfortable while telling your story? Do you feel you have to tell more or less than the truth? Do you think you are getting the straight scoop from each interviewer?

If the interviewer makes you feel uneasy, this might well signal a personality mismatch. But if you sense that things are going right—that you and the interviewer "click"—then perhaps you have found the right company and the right decision maker.

Dos and don'ts when answering questions

1. Be prepared.
2. Listen.
3. Make sure you understand the question completely. If you don't, ask the interviewer either to repeat the question or to rephrase it.
4. Answer questions in a succinct, frank, and to-the-point manner.
5. Think carefully about your answers. For your own sake (and the interviewer's) don't just blurt out anything. A little pause can be very effective and impressive.
6. Don't overanswer questions or overexplain and don't say any more than is necessary.
7. Don't answer questions with a simple "yes" or "no." Explain your answers, but within reason.
8. Don't assume that you understand a poorly worded question and then try to answer it. You may end up confusing the interviewer as well as yourself.

More about questions

An interviewer who doesn't ask you questions is telling you one of two things:

1. You've covered everything the interviewer wants to know about you.
2. You blew it. You might just as well forget the whole thing and go home.

Also, if an interviewer starts asking you for names of other people in your field (which is unprofessional and improper), it is time for you to leave. You aren't there to help anyone but yourself. Go back home and try again another day.

As you've seen, professionals use questions to determine your interests, attitudes, and ability to contribute. They're trying to project you into that position.

Here's one final bit of advice about your answers: When answering a question, instead of saying, "I feel," "I think," "I guess," or "I hope," make a positive comment: "I *know* I can . . ." (if it's true).

How about questions on your part?

At the beginning of the interview, you tried to help the interviewer direct the questions properly, but now you want to get some in-depth answers yourself. I've found that sample questions on the next few pages are helpful. I'm sure you can think of many others. Also, you may have asked a number of questions during the consulting interview that you did not get answers to. Start with those of major interest to you and then you might try some of the following ones.

Remember that throughout your questioning, there is nothing wrong in asking the interviewer to go into detail, to define such-and-such a term or phrase because you don't understand it, or even to expand on some things which aren't clear and to the point.

A word of caution is necessary here. Your questions *must* come before your sales pitch to the company. Why? If you don't get the answers to them, you might end up with a case of "foot-in-mouth" disease (saying the wrong thing) that enters a terminal phase in a matter of seconds or minutes.

I have broken the sample questions into the following categories:

1. Questions about the company and its people
2. Questions about the position
3. Questions about the company's products or services
4. Questions about the company's sales and marketing efforts
5. Questions about the company's customers
6. Questions about the industry
7. Miscellaneous questions

Of course, these are only suggested questions. Go over the list carefully and choose the ones that fit you. You can't possibly ask all of them, nor would it be appropriate to do so.

Questions about the company and its people

1. What organizational changes might be required if I were to accept this position?

2. How would the people affected react to this situation, and how would I be involved before joining the company? During the transition? After joining the company?
3. How would you be involved in these changes?
4. Could I have your permission to speak personally with other people in the company regarding their likes and dislikes and their outlook for the company as well as the opportunities it has to offer?
5. What is the most common reason people leave this industry? This company? This position?
6. Would I fit into the team as to temperament and personality?
7. Could I see a copy of your organization chart showing this position in relation to others in the company?
8. Could you tell me something about the other top people in the company—their goals, aspirations, and potential?
9. How much of the personality of the chief executive is reflected throughout the company? Could you go into some detail regarding this?
10. You've told me many of the positives regarding the company. How about some of the negatives?
11. Does this company hire relatives and friends of people in management?
12. If that is the case, is this hiring done for key positions?
13. Where is your company heading?
14. What expansion efforts are you making at present?
15. Is the "marketing concept" practiced in your company? To what extent?
16. What, specifically, is your corporate objective? What are your corporate goals?
17. What are you doing to attract new and dynamic talent to your company and to this industry?
18. Is promotion strictly from within? Why?
19. What kind of backup support does the company provide to [whatever position you're aiming at] in the resolution of complaints? How much emphasis is placed on customer service and satisfying customer needs and problems?
20. What is your company doing to protect and expand its position in the industry?
21. Could you tell me something about this division and its overall contributions to the profits of the company?
22. Do you anticipate getting a promotion or being transferred within the next six months?

23. Could I see a copy of your organization chart to get a feeling for your corporate structure?
24. Who are some of the other top people in the company? Could you tell me something about them professionally?
25. How did they climb up the ladder?
26. What are some of their backgrounds and accomplishments?
27. What are the expansion plans of your company?
28. Could you tell me something about your [whichever department you are interested in] and its goals?
29. What do you dislike about this industry? This company?

Questions about the position

1. Why is the position available?
2. How long has the position been open? Why?
3. Why did the previous person leave?
4. How long do most people last in this position with your company?
5. What would be expected of me as the new _____ in the short term? The intermediate term? The long term?
6. What are the long-range prospects for this position in terms of professional growth and promotional opportunities?
7. What are the company's expansion plans, and where might I fit into these plans?
8. What flexibility in departmental or company decisions would I have?
9. How much control would I have?
10. What is the relationship of authority to responsibility in this position?
11. What will be the lines of communication between you and me?
12. Could you tell me something about the educational requirements of such a position?
13. Does your company look for educational credentials, proved performance, or both?
14. Could you give me a copy of the job description outlining the duties and responsibilities of the position, or could you give me a rundown of these yourself?
15. How would you describe above-average performance in this position?
16. What importance do you place on a high GPA during college?

17. What importance is placed on extracurricular activities during college? On activities outside the office?
18. Could you tell me something about the personality requirements of this position?
19. How much travel is required?
20. Will relocation be required within the next five years?
21. Could you tell me something about hours—your concern for getting the specific job done versus clock punching, etc.?
22. Could you tell me about your initial training program and your ongoing training program? How extensive are these programs?
23. What can you offer that is more advantageous than what your competitors offer?
24. What kind of people do you look for in your [department you are interested in] in this company?
25. Could you give me an example of your typical [title] development program over a five-year period?

Questions about the company's products or services

1. How many products are you currently promoting?
2. Do you have many products which are being phased out? Why?
3. What new products do you anticipate introducing to the marketplace? Can you tell me about them? When will they be introduced?
4. Can your current sales and marketing staff handle these products effectively?
5. What kind of research techniques do you use in checking out a product or service for your efforts?
6. What efforts are made regarding follow-up as to product efficacy and product quality?
7. Has your company sought additional marketing outlets such as direct-mail efforts, catalogs, and direct selling techniques?
8. Are you doing anything to upgrade your current products, such as using different packaging or making design changes?
9. How compatible are your product lines? Do they provide for synergism? Why?
10. Are you attempting to add other products which will allow for this?

11. How closely is your product line related to the ups and downs of the economy?
12. Who are some of your major competitors?
13. How do their prices compare with yours?
14. What are some of your competitors' problems?
15. How does your company avoid these problems or overcome them?
16. What are some of the major problems you're facing now? Are these current or ongoing problems?[8]

Questions about the company's sales and marketing efforts

1. What is your marketing plan for selling your company as well as its products?
2. Do you have a company marketing brochure along with sales brochures?
3. Do you have business development letters, etc.?
4. How much emphasis do you put on phone selling? Personal selling?
5. How closely do you follow your marketing plan?
6. How frequently is the marketing plan reviewed as to effectiveness?
7. Have there been any major recent changes in the marketing plan?
8. How flexible is your marketing plan?
9. Could you tell me something about your media efforts? Which agency assists you in this regard?

Questions about the company's customers

1. Do you have formal (contractual) or informal relationships with your customers?
2. How much research do you do regarding potential customers before you accept them as customers?
3. Do your customers provide you with feedback? How is this done? Do you seek this information or do anything to acquire it?
4. Do you provide your customers with feedback about them?
5. Do you assist customers in designing their advertising literature?

[8]Most of your efforts will be aimed at this question. Delve deeply to find the problem areas in which you can uniquely contribute.

6. What are your personal and professional opinions of your customer base? Why do you feel this way?
7. How do you think you could improve this relationship?
8. What do you do to ensure that your salespeople gain the greatest customer exposure time?
9. Could you provide me with some examples of sales literature, product literature, catalogs, etc.?
10. What major customers do you have in your customer base? Why? Who aren't you selling to? Why?

Questions about the industry

1. What kind of relationship do you enjoy with your competitors?
2. What are the major breakdowns of types of companies in your industry?
3. Could you tell me something about profit margins in the industry?
4. Where is your company on this scale? Why?
5. What are some of the alternative solutions you've identified in regard to industrywide problems?
6. What are you trying to achieve in this industry?
7. What do you think is the growth potential within this industry, and how does your company view its future and potential within this industry? Why?
8. Are there any major life-style changes which you can foresee as threatening this industry?
9. Do you anticipate any major competition from foreign companies?
10. Could you tell me something about the salary levels in this industry? How about incentives programs?

Miscellaneous questions

1. Is your company a member of a trade association?
2. Do your executives take an active part in these association activities?
3. In which demographic areas are you concentrating your efforts at present? Why?
4. What other areas are you planning to expand to? How soon? Why?
5. Are you planning any cutbacks? Why?
6. Do you attend national or regional trade shows?
7. Do you consider these to be of major value? Why?
8. Why have you been able to make it to the top in this company and this industry when others haven't?

9. How often is your authority usurped by higher management?
10. Could you tell me something about budgets and purchase orders within the company? Is there needless concern with small expenditures?
11. Are there any questions I should have asked and didn't?
12. What exactly is your position with the company? What are your duties and responsibilities?
13. What are your professional aspirations?
14. How have you been able to succeed in this industry on a continuing basis? This is such a tough industry.
15. What have been some of your major contributions to this company? To this industry?
16. If a person were to come to your company and suggest specific ways of solving many of the problems we've discussed today, who would have the authority to hire that person?

Obviously, one of the main reasons for asking questions like these is to demonstrate to the interviewer your capabilities and your interest in the position and the company. Simply stated, the fact that you are prepared and have so many of the right questions tells the interviewer that you might be able to come up with a lot of the right answers as well.

Again, throughout all your questioning don't forget to show a genuine interest in the interviewer—his or her past, background, and experience. Remember to be a good listener, even during your sell part of the interview.

Your sales pitch to the company

It is your goal and your responsibility to tell the interviewer what the company needs and why it needs you. After all questions, yours and the interviewer's, have been answered, you must continue to close the sale by helping the interviewer "buy" you on the basis of the benefits you can provide.

If you are discussing a specific position, confirm that you understand what it is. If necessary, review your understanding of the position with the interviewer. Be sure to ask for as much information *in writing* as possible. If no specific position is being discussed, the onus will be on you to create—with the interviewer—a position (as I've been saying all along). Either way, you must prove to the interviewer that you are the finest candidate he or she has ever interviewed. Everything you've done to prepare for this interview will make that possible.

Problems and more problems

As I stated earlier, problems are simply opportunities looking for solutions. In all your research and interviewing, one of your most important concerns is to uncover problems—to identify opportunities. The main reason for this is to arm you so that you'll know what you're getting into *before* you're there. It also enables you to determine for yourself whether you are ready and able to handle the problems and challenges.

However, you should not be so presumptuous as to think that you're going to be able to enter Company X and immediately solve its problems. Nor should you make interviewing time problem-solving time. For example, perhaps in your efforts to find out about this company you've discovered problems that even the company itself might not have been aware of. Be extremely cautious here. You must be careful not to step on too many toes, not to make tidal waves. This is still problem-discovery time, not problem-solving time. Don't say, "I heard, while doing research, that your company is run by a bunch of bastards—that they don't do this and that, they don't follow through on their promises, etc." Instead, use this information to formulate additional insightful questions, such as: "What are management's techniques for handling problem accounts?" and "How are customer problems handled, and by whom?"

Start the sale

Be warm and sincere. *Show your character.* Tell how your background, education, and abilities qualify you perfectly for the position. Discuss your career goals. Explain how you can achieve these goals sooner if you take this position with the company than you would otherwise.

Use your notes to point out specific areas of your knowledge and ability. In talking about yourself, refer to your profile. Don't be so strong that you sound as if you have a chip on your shoulder, but certainly show self-confidence. Be succint and to the point. Don't get involved in long personal discussions; both you and the interviewer might lose track of the original thought. Be proud of your knowledge and accomplishments. If you aren't out there tooting your horn, just who do you think will be?

Remember that companies are buying five benefits when they buy you:
1. Your moneymaking (money-saving) ability
2. Your knowledge and contacts
3. Your potential to produce results

4. Your proved abilities
5. Your personality

Be careful when bragging about yourself. However, unless you think you're great, how can you expect someone else to think so? I've found that the following statements are effective. But again, use caution. Don't say anything about yourself that you can't say honestly.

1. "I'm a people motivator." (Can you imagine saying this, only to find that you have motivated the interviewer to fall asleep?)
2. "I have a high energy level." (What would happen if the next thing out of your mouth was a yawn or if your posture showed that you directed most of your energy toward relaxing in a prone position? Enough said? Here are some more.)
3. "I'm flexible in my thinking."
4. "I'm an extrovert; I like people."
5. "I'm a money-maker."
6. "I'm success-motivated and goal-oriented."
7. "I'm a doer, not a talker."
8. "I have a lot of raw, undeveloped talent."
9. "I'm a creator of circumstance rather than a creature of circumstance."
10. "I possess a great deal of persistence and determination."
11. "I'm ambitious."
12. "I learn fast and retain well what I learn."
13. "I'm intelligent and knowledgeable, especially in this field."
14. "I'm career-oriented."
15. "I've chosen this field. I want to be the best in it because it is the best field for me."
16. "I like the atmosphere and environment of this field."
17. "I'm well respected by my peers and by many people in this industry."
18. "I'm dedicated to achievement."
19. "I want and like to be involved."
20. "I don't make waves; I listen and evaluate."

Nothing sells like enthusiasm! Enthusiasm is contagious. Make the interviewer enthusiastic about your skills and abilities and your potential for identifying and solving problems—in short, enthusiastic about having you in the position you desire—your niche.

You must also send out good vibrations—vibrations that say, "I like this person, and this person likes me." It's always a good idea to stroke both the company's ego and the interviewer's ego. Compliment and recognize known corporate achievements and those of management. Flattery can't hurt, but be truthful. Give credit only where it's due.

Continue the sale

Believe in yourself and show that you do.

Tell about your preparation for the interview.

Talk about the company's products or services and about what you know of the company and its successes (forget the failures).

Tell of your past experience and how this position is a natural continuation of all your efforts to date (for example, jobs during college, college preparation for this field, on-the-job experience while in college, recent positions in this industry, avocations relating to this field and this industry, and activities proving leadership ability).

Tell how you've built a foundation for your entire future career and how this position fits into your plans and goals.

Tell why you're turned on by the company.

Put the idea into the interviewer's head that you are "the person" the company wants and needs to hire—that you have the ability and the unique talent to fill the position better than anyone else could. Prove your uniqueness!

Don'ts of the follow-up interview

1. Don't discuss money. Your most important concern is opportunity—the opportunity for advancement, training, and experience in your chosen career.
2. Don't discuss the make, color, and optional equipment of the company car.
3. Don't discuss religious beliefs, racial concerns, or political leanings.
4. Don't discuss the company retirement plan (unless you're within five years of being eligible—then do so with caution).
5. Don't discuss unimportant incidentals of the specific position's perquisites.
6. Don't discuss problems you had with your former employer. Always protect your former (or present) employer's confidence. Interviews are not the time for bad-mouthing anybody or anything.
7. Don't discuss vacations.

8. Don't discuss sick leave.

Use good common sense. You'll have the opportunity to go over all the important considerations at the hiring interview during the salary-negotiation part—*if* you do a good job at each of the follow-up interviews.

More don'ts

1. Don't allow yourself to be interviewed by anyone but a decision maker—initially, that is.
2. Don't allow telephone interviews. They're deadly.
3. Don't allow two, three, or more people to interview you at one time. The interview will turn into an inquisition.
4. Don't accept an offer made at a follow-up interview.
5. Don't accept the offer of a position lower than the one which you are seeking—you *know* what you can do.
6. Don't allow an excessive number of phone calls and other interruptions to upset you. If the interviewer is so inconsiderate as to permit the disturbances, it's not your fault.
7. Don't allow yourself to be intimidated by the atmosphere, the impressive offices, etc.

You say you're still concerned about the money situation and wonder what to do if the interviewer wants to discuss money. If the interviewer insists on trying to find out what salary level you expect, say something like, "I prefer not to discuss money at this time. What's more important is. . . ." However, if the interviewer really pushes, you must mention a fair figure or a fair dollar range. (This is really supposed to be part of the hiring interview, however, which is discussed in Chapter 14.)

"But what about the great things I've done?"

In the chapters on the informal consulting interview, no mention was made of your contributions to former employers. This subject should be saved for the formal interview. Be aware of the importance of timing; this is when you bring in the very best part of your sales pitch. And so another commandment: *Thou shalt be prepared to discuss major contributions you've made to former employers, unique contributions you can make to this company and this industry, and legitimate reasons for wanting this specific position.*[9] These should be specifics, not generalities. Let's look at some examples.

---

[9]About five contributions of each type and about five reasons for wanting a specific position should suffice.

Contributions to former employers

1. Developed a new product line—projected sales this year, 442,000 cases; projected profits, $482,000
2. Developed new department which is projected within four years to represent in excess of 52 percent of total company sales
3. Sold the single largest order ever shipped to one account: 88,000 cases
4. Attained 114 new-product authorizations in a four-month period
5. My accounts received "Retailer of the Year" awards for three consecutive years
6. Generated $122 million in sales during my nine years as sales manager
7. Directed activities of 1,100 sales representatives
8. Achieved national recognition for sales programs and new marketing techniques
9. Created fourteen new markets—sales value, $26 million
10. Developed and monitored sales and profit plan allowing savings in excess of $4.7 million annually

Potential contributions to this company

1. Successfully increase penetration of current product lines in the market
2. Develop marketing concepts by demographic area
3. Define and project short-term, intermediate-term, and long-term goals and incorporate them into a specific plan of action
4. Identify problems indigenous to this industry and turn these opportunities into successful, moneymaking solutions
5. Communicate and motivate company, broker, and key trade personnel
6. Increase sales and market penetration
7. Design, develop, and implement new and innovative marketing concepts
8. Provide greater market coverage through improved training and motivation
9. Accomplish sales and marketing objectives while maintaining optimum profitability through intelligent cost control
10. Develop an esprit de corps among your staff to achieve sales successes, thereby gaining recognition for individuals and the company

I suggest that you type your lists of contributions and give the interviewer a copy so that he or she may review them with you and ask questions as you both go along. Remember that figures are very meaningful to all business people. Be as specific as possible. Also be sure to note all the interviewer's questions and concerns so that you may answer them in detail in your performance description.

When speaking about your potential contributions, say that you'd like to give the interviewer a complete and detailed description of them in about a week and that this is why you've asked for a copy of the job description (the subject of the next chapter).

The closing

The actual sale

It's been said that a sale actually begins when the customer says "No." There is some truth to this, but don't get carried away by it.

I've found a number of "closes" to be quite effective. The whole idea behind these closes is to find out what the interviewer likes and dislikes about your background and experience. You must get the interviewer to verbalize these feelings so that you can be aware of them and deal with them.

You must also show that you're vitally concerned about this position and what it can mean to your career—and your future. Here are some examples of closes that you might use.

Close 1: "Now that you know who I am, I'm sure you can understand why I'm interested in the position and why I'm qualified. Where do we go from here?"

Close 2: "It seems as if I'm the person you're looking for. Don't you agree?"

Close 3: "I want you to hire me because of the person I can be with your company and in this position."

Close 4: "Do you feel you know me well enough to make a decision? I've made my decision."

Close 5: You've been able to determine from your interviews that four or five major factors are important in the decision to hire. In a very pleasant and positive manner, address yourself to each of these. For example, "Do I have the corporate image you're seeking?" "Is my background satisfactory?" "Are my industry and customer contacts in line with your needs and requirements?" "Do I have the managerial abilities you're seeking?"

If the interviewer has a negative reaction to one of these questions, say something like, "OK, then, we've got to work on that one."

Besides contributions to former employers and potential contributions to this company, you should also mention legitimate reasons why you want this position. Here are some examples:

1. "I want this position because there is only one company like yours in this industry, and I want to hitch my wagon to your star."
2. "I want my name to be identified with a top organization—your organization. This will help me to become more successful. Your company name and reputation will enable me to be the person I want to be."
3. "This position will enable me to deal with my own type of people."
4. "This position will allow me to be the person I really am."
5. "I identify with the product, the company, the industry, and you. I know that we could work together very effectively."
6. "This position will satisfy my needs as to prestige, utilization of my skills and abilities, salary, and so forth."

If that's not enough

By this time, if the interviewer hasn't suggested that you meet with other executives who would support your being hired, you should ask to be referred to someone who might be interested in having you work for the company. You're pushing for a close, but in a professional manner. It is always easy to say "no" in any situation; thus you should try to avoid providing the interviewer with any "no"-type opportunities. However, if the interviewer says "no" after all your efforts, you must take the referral approach.

By using the referral approach, you'll be keeping open the important lines of communication which you've worked so hard to create. Here's an example of how this might work:

> Thanks very much for your time. I appreciate your helping me to better understand this industry and your company. I can well appreciate your current situation as you've outlined it, and I'm sorry that we couldn't get together. However, now that we've had a chance to get to know each other, perhaps you might suggest one or two companies in this industry where I might fit in.

Here's what you'll be accomplishing with this approach:

1. Making the best of a bad situation
2. Proving your professionalism—your acumen
3. Complimenting the interviewer by asking for assistance and advice

4. Showing the interviewer a way out of a touchy situation
5. Making a professional friend and establishing a contact in one of the industries of your choice

Answers during the interview

We have discussed all the parts of the formal interview except how you go about answering questions during this type of interview. First, remember that there's no place for negatives in your makeup, much less in the interview situation; this should be a totally positive experience. Turn any and all negatives into positives. For example:

> INTERVIEWER: You seem to be very security-oriented.
> YOU: I'm fully aware that the only real security there is in life is the security that I make for myself and my family on a day-to-day basis.
> INTERVIEWER: What were your reasons for leaving your former employer?
> YOU: I felt that my goals had been accomplished and that I had nothing further to contribute.
> INTERVIEWER: What are your goals in life?
> YOU: Do you mean my personal goals or my professional goals? Do you want to know about my goals in the short term or the long term?

As you can see from the above questions and answers, you must keep things on a positive and straightforward basis. When you're asked a general question, you should try to determine specifically what the interviewer is trying to find out. Give honest answers which you feel comfortable about. Refer to the answers you prepared for exercises earlier in the chapter.

Handling objections

Objections are just like questions or problems: They're merely opportunities looking for solutions.

Remember to try to incorporate in all your answers your concerns with the benefits you can provide to the company in the form of:

1. Profits
2. Savings
3. Growth

Show that you are concerned with what you can do for the company, not with what the company can do for you. Show that you're not running from something, but advancing toward something: your niche.

How many interviews can you expect to go through?

Most companies require each candidate to have three to five interviews before a final decision is reached. You must prepare for additional interviews in much the same way as you prepared for the first one.

Remember that every person you meet who is in any way affiliated with the company is an individual and must be sold on you and your potential. Each person concerned with your hiring has unique "hot buttons" which you must identify. Thus, every time you meet a new person in the company (secretary, janitor, or whatever), treat that person as an individual—as you'd like to be treated. You must handle each interview as a new sale, i.e., use the same interview format—right from the beginning.

There is a very good chance that most of the people you meet will know nothing about you, or very little at best. Don't assume that each has been given a complete rundown on you.

What can you expect at the second, third, and fourth interviews?

Here's what you can expect at those follow-up interviews with the decision maker and others in the company:
1. A review of first-interview questions and answers and those not covered during the consulting or follow-up interview
2. A question-and-answer session regarding additional thoughts and concerns
3. A possible introduction to others in the company, such as the interviewer's boss or your potential coworkers
4. Confirmation of your interest in the company and the company's interest in you

Remember that each new person you meet—regardless of position or title—will be critically appraising you and perhaps providing feedback about you. Be at your best.

Score sheets

Because interviewers see so many candidates, many of them keep a score sheet on which they record their immediate impressions during and after the interview. Unless these impressions are recorded, they will soon drift into oblivion. Figure 4 shows a typical evaluation score sheet.

Your impressions are also important. After an interview, you should record all your thoughts and ideas. The following list of questions will help you do this:

1. What did I like about the company? The industry? The decision maker (interviewer)? The environment? The corporate personality? The corporate philosophy?
2. What did I dislike about each of the above?

TRAXEL ASSOCIATES, INC.
THE PROFESSIONAL EXECUTIVE SEARCH FIRM

CANDIDATE INTERVIEW EVALUATION SHEET

Name of applicant : _____ Time : _____
Date : _____

	Good	Average	Poor
1. Appearance	___	___	___
2. Preparation for interview	___	___	___
3. Human relations skills	___	___	___
4. Stability	___	___	___
5. Reaction to stress situation	___	___	___
6. Enthusiasm	___	___	___
7. Verbal abilities	___	___	___
8. Knowledge of industry	___	___	___
9. Success motivation	___	___	___
10. Goal orientation	___	___	___
11. Money–making potential	___	___	___
12. People orientation	___	___	___
13. Ambition level	___	___	___
14. Self–confidence	___	___	___
15. Warmth and sincerity	___	___	___
16. Persistence and determination	___	___	___
17. Insight	___	___	___
18. Relevancy	___	___	___
19. Creativity	___	___	___
20. Intellectual qualities	___	___	___

Personal remarks : _____

_____

Fig. 4

3. Have my impressions changed any since that first meeting?
4. Did each interviewer give me a good overview of his or her position and of the company and the industry in relation to that position?
5. If not, what could I have done, or what will I do, to correct this?
6. Which questions weren't answered during the interview? Were they important? Should I include these in the next interview?
7. Should I rearrange these questions so they'll flow better?
8. Are there any additional questions I should have asked?
9. What successes did I achieve? How can I capitalize on these?
10. What mistakes did I make? Where did I go wrong?
11. Was my preparation for the interview adequate? Where should I have placed greater emphasis?
12. What was my reaction to this situation? Am I ready to go ahead with more interviews, or do I need to do more research?
13. Are there other things that I could have done or said that might have proved helpful?
14. Could I really do an outstanding job for that company?
15. Could I work with and for that person?
16. What are the chances that I will be able to utilize my skills fully in this company? In this industry?
17. What is my growth potential in this industry and this company?
18. Is this truly the company, industry, and position for me?

You can probably add questions of your own to this list.

It's the follow-up that counts

Now it's time to introduce the *pièce de résistance.* Take all your ammunition—the "hot buttons" you've discovered, the opportunities you've uncovered, and your knowledge of the company and the industry—and put it into a *performance description* that tells how you would go about methodically defining and solving problems for this decision maker and this company. This is what follow-up—the subject of Chapter 12—is all about. Follow-up is also what decision makers have in mind when they say, "Why don't you put something together for us on paper, and we'll give it serious consideration?"

ELEVEN

The View from the Other Side

Let's look at you from the other side of the desk—the decision maker's side. Let's try to get a feeling for what the interviewer will be thinking and for how each decision maker will be looking at you.[1]

As I stated at the beginning of the last chapter, *the goal of interviewing is selection,* and *the goal of selection is prediction.* Again, decision makers are trying to determine which person or persons will have the greatest potential to contribute to the growth and success of their organization. They are seeking to ferret out the information that will enable them to evaluate and predict your potential for success within their organization.

How does an interviewer evaluate you?

Decision makers use a number of devices to assist them in evaluating you before, during, and after each interview. Let's discuss each of these time periods.

---

[1]Note that this chapter, like Chap. 10, is concerned solely with *formal interviewing procedures* (the follow-up interview, etc.), and the techniques described here are not to be confused with those set forth for the *informal consulting interview,* which is the subject of Chaps. 6–9.

Before the interview

Before the interview, the knowledgeable interviewer will review your profile, résumé, and/or application. He or she will be checking the following points.

Overall neatness and appearance: Are there any misspelled words (a major pet peeve)? Is it neatly typed and professional in appearance? Does it look appealing?

Is it specific or generalized?: Do you have a definite idea of where you are going (position-desired section)? Are you looking for something specific? Do you really know what you want?

Address changes: Are they frequent? Why? Is this saying something about your stability? Penciled-in changes on top of résumés aren't acceptable.

Only one position: Do you seem to be unwilling to take risks or try new things? Are you satisfied until circumstances force you to make a change?

Numerous positions?: Is there a logical progression as to positions, or are the positions you have held unrelated, showing lack of career planning and goal orientation?

Is it predictive?: Does it detail unique and potential areas for contribution, concentrate on past performance alone, or simply note positions with no contributions?

Current address: Is your current address in a good neighborhood? Do you live in a house or an apartment? Do you live above your means? If so, how is this possible?

Marital status: If you are single, this may mean that you just aren't ready to settle down yet. A recent separation or divorce may indicate problems. However, being single or divorced could be a major asset if a substantial amount of travel is required.

Family situation: If you are happily married and family-oriented, this almost guarantees stability. Are you motivated to get out and do the job? Does your family take an active interest in your profession? Is your family too large for the income the company can offer? Will moonlighting be required?

Other income: Does your wife or husband work? If so, how much do you depend on this income? Is additional income needed from another source to maintain living standards? Do you depend on your family for additional income?

Father's occupation: If your parents have a business, will you be joining it? Will you be taking it over or assisting with it on a part-time basis (while on the company payroll)?

Education: Is it adequate for the position? (Not every person hired needs to have the qualifications to become a company president.) Is your schooling completed? If not, why? Is this also indicative of your ability to carry through?

Outside activities: Does your participation evidence leadership and effort? How involved do you get? Do these activities lend themselves to this business and position?

College major: Is your education relevant to the requirements of this position? Does this show career preparation? Does it show that you might be using this job as a bridge or a temporary situation to gain additional training and education?

Work history: Have there been any extended periods of unemployment? If so, what were the circumstances? Gaps in employment could be a danger signal. Self-employment can be both good and bad, depending on company personality requirements.

Earnings history: Does this show steady progress? Is it realistic for your current position? If your income in the last position was 15 percent more than the top of the current budgeted salary for the position, the employer is playing with fire.

Reasons for leaving last employer: Are they plausible? Will there also be "personality conflict" in the new position? If you left to seek a "better opportunity," does this mean that you are continually moving to better yourself instead of striving to grow within an organization?

Special comments: Do you show good business acumen and have good reasons for wanting the position? Do you take extra time to go into detail, thus showing your initiative?

Many other factors can be identified through inspection of candidate-submitted forms. But forms are merely tools. Your face-to-face meetings are the most important element in the hiring decision. All the additional information about you that the interviewer has is merely supportive of his or her positive or negative impressions formed during these meetings.

During the interview

The decision maker's businesslike and somewhat impersonal demeanor reflects the fact that he or she is trying to avoid judging you on the basis of personal feelings and emotions.

If some of your comments and statements seem contradictory, the interviewer may probe more deeply to discover the reasons for this. He or she is checking on that all-important factor—your integrity.

Don't be offended because the interviewer asks a lot of questions. Interviewers want as many insights and facts as possible so that they will be able to make an informed decision. The further they probe, the greater their interest.

The knowledgeable interviewer will consider three personality categories during the interview: your attitude—whether you will do the job; your ability—whether you can do the job; your character—whether, in doing the job, you will or will not observe the rules. Let's discuss each of these in detail.

Your attitude

The interviewer will be assessing your attitude during the entire interview. He or she will concentrate (consciously or subconsciously) on the following:

Enthusiasm: This is number one in importance. Are you enthusiastic about the position and about yourself in it? Do you ask knowledgeable questions? Are they relevant and pertinent? Are you passive and indifferent, or does your enthusiasm come across and make the interviewer enthusiastic?

Personality: Do you seem to be overbearing, conceited, a know-it-all, and perhaps overly aggressive, or are you the opposite? Do you have the personality required for the position? Are you persistent? Determined?

Posture, demeanor, and bearing: Are you poised during the interview, or do you seem nervous and unsure of yourself?

Outlook: Are you career-oriented, goal-oriented, and success-motivated? Have you planned your career and does this position seem to fit in with your plans? Why?

Preparation: Are you prepared for the interview? Have you done research on the company, the industry, and the products prior to the interview? In how much depth?

Empathy and rapport: Are you warm and sincere? Do you speak and react with feeling, interest, and concern?

Concern with detail: Are you conscientious and concerned with detail? How do you feel about hard work? Follow-up?

Disposition: Do you seem to be a happy person or the depressed type?

Your ability

In addition to your attitude, the interviewer will also be concerned with your proved or demonstrated performance to date. He or she will be concentrating on the following:

Verbal skills: Do you express yourself clearly and succinctly, or do you have difficulty making a point? Your ability to use complex sentences will be indicative of your verbal skills. However, a good vocabulary isn't necessarily a sign of intelligence.

Confidence: Are you confident of your ability in this industry and with these types of products? What is this confidence based on?

Training: Is your training applicable to the industry and its products, or do you have the ability to learn quickly, so that this isn't of major importance?

Experience and skills: Is your experience applicable? Do you seem to have the skills necessary to do the job?

Problems: Are there unfavorable factors in your record? If so, do you discuss these openly, or do you make excuses and seem overly defensive?

Intellect: Do you become overly involved in specifics, or do you speak in generalities? (Discussing generalities is indicative of intelligence, i.e., an ability to see the forest in spite of the trees).

Alertness: Are you alert? Do you catch on quickly?

Analytical ability: Do you analyze, define, and state problems clearly, or do you merely accept solutions?

Logic: Do you discuss a subject in a logical, step-by-step manner?

Intuitiveness: Do you grasp a situation without having to have all the facts?

Creativity: Are you willing to try new approaches? Does one idea lead you to a new and better approach? Do you offer more than one solution to a problem?

Skills: Do you have the necessary skills relating to people, data, and things? To which level in the skills hierarchy have you progressed? Do your skills match the requirements of the job?

Knowledge: Is your knowledge applicable to the job?

Competitiveness: Have you been active in sports? Do you take an active or passive interest at this time? Are you a team player or a loner?

Your character

"A chain is only as strong as its weakest link." If a weakness exists in any of these three links—attitude, ability, or character—this will imperil your chances, initially and on an ongoing basis. Here's what the interviewer will be looking for as to your character:

Integrity: Are you honest and straightforward? Do you look the interviewer squarely in the eyes when answering questions?

Stability: Are you contradictory in your answers? Your attitudes? Does your past work history show that you lack stability or perhaps are overly stable?

Attitude toward money: Do you overemphasize money, or do you strike the proper balance between opportunity and money? Is your salary history consistent with positions held?

Directness: Do you talk around a subject instead of coming to the point? Do you make a lot of excuses?

Maturity: How do you speak about former employers? If you condemn them, what will you be doing while working with this company? Do you use "hip" language, slang words, and so on, indicating immaturity and the need to impress?

Responsibility: Have you demonstrated a willingness to accept responsibility, such as for children and a home? Are you an active participant in community-oriented activities?

Other factors:

Loyalty
Temperament
Disposition
Humor
Reputation
Moral constitution
Ethical standards
Principles
Individuality
Cooperativeness

After the interview

After the interview, you might be saying, "That was great; my hard work has paid off. Thank you, Robert Traxel!" Or you might be thinking, "I'm not quite sure how I came across. The interviewer was pleasant, communicative, and very nice, but he was mysterious—there was something missing. I can't quite put my finger on it, but I'm not sure where I stand with him." Or maybe you'll say, "Boy, did I bomb out on that one!"

What will the interviewer be thinking?

If you are one of a number of candidates interviewed that day, the interviewer might record his or her impressions of you on a candidate evaluation score sheet, make additional notes and add these to your supporting documentation, and then go on to the next candidate.

If no other candidate was seen that day, your only competition for the interviewer's thoughts will be his or her normal hassles and problems. Positive and negative thoughts about the meeting—about your experience, qualifications, personality, and potential—will keep popping up in the interviewer's mind. These will reinforce the interviewer's initial feelings and impressions and those gained during this formal follow-up interview.

If the interviewer likes you, the following concerns will be important:

1. Does he or she identify with you and feel comfortable with you?
2. Exactly *where* will you fit into the organization?
3. Specifically, why does the company need you?
4. How can your talents, skills, and abilities be best utilized?
5. Could you be an asset to the organization?

In the next few chapters we'll discuss further steps in your search for the right position—your niche.

TWELVE

The Performance Description

As I said in an earlier chapter, it's important for you to "service" yourself into the right position.

You have now given the decision makers in the companies that interest you an opportunity to see you in person and you have provided them with your personal profile. The questions you've asked and the answers you've provided have been honest, straightforward, and to the point. The decision makers now have most of the facts they need to make an intelligent and knowledgeable decision.

Now let's introduce the next concept: the performance description. The performance description is a combination of the job description and the person description, which will be explained in detail shortly. While the personal profile tells decision makers *who* you are, the performance description tells them *what* you are able to do and *where, why, and how* you can make the greatest contributions.

Follow-up ingredients

In the marketing and sales fields, experts emphasize five important factors necessary for the promotion and sale of a product or service:

1. Continuing research
2. Advertising
3. Packaging
4. Follow-up
5. Service

These five factors are more important in selling a product than perhaps all others put together. This chapter is concerned with how to put these five important factors together to promote you into the right position.

You have gone out on consulting interviews and follow-up interviews, you have submitted profiles, you have been doing research, and you have been gaining exposure (advertising, promoting, and selling). Now comes the important element of closing that sale—the final packaging and follow-up.

Because much of this book is aimed at executives and aspiring managers, you, in your packaging, must be able to prove that you are worthy of being called a "pro"—that you can handle the money and the responsibilities that go along with a managerial position. You must also be able to prove your ability to *define, demonstrate,* and *communicate.*

Somebody else's house

Imagine how you'd feel if you were asked to live in someone else's house, with all that person's furniture, clothing, personal effects, and so on. Although it would be difficult at the beginning, eventually you'd learn to adapt. Still, you'd prefer a house that reflected your own ideas, tastes, likes, and dislikes—a house where you'd really feel comfortable and "at home."

Now ask yourself where you spend the majority of your working hours—the majority of your life. Isn't it terribly important to spend these hours in a position (a home) where you feel comfortable and where your skills and talents can be appreciated and utilized to their fullest? Your performance description—related directly to your abilities, attitudes, and character (i.e., your personality), as well as your potential to perform—can be of great value in helping you find such a position.

Let's start at the beginning

First, you must have a product to package—you. You started your research regarding that product in Chapter 3, and you have put together your personal profile. Now you must do some additional research on yourself as the final step toward creating the customized position you desire—your niche.

It is my belief that there is an inherent flaw in the traditional concept of the job description. The flaw is that the description is written by someone other than the person who actually performs the job—for example, by:

1. The personnel manager
2. A creative secretary
3. A management consultant
4. A personnel staff member who adapted the description from a book on management systems
5. A concerned manager who is interested in helping trainees get off to a good start

In four out of the five cases above, the odds are against there being any room for realism or practicality in the job description. For the most part, it has to be thought of as a good exercise, nicely written, and full of glowing goals, but lacking in reality. Yet a job description is demanding, idealistic, and all-encompassing. We can come to three conclusions about it:

1. It is somewhat instructive (for new employees), but it is also threatening, frustrating, and overly idealistic.
2. Although it impresses management, it isn't necessarily motivational and impressive to the people who need it most.
3. It is totally lacking in definition of unique personality factors such as skills, talents, and abilities.

The job description fails because it has to be all things to all people concerned. It leaves little room for flexibility and self-expression. It is fine and somewhat effective for entry-level people, but for executives, manager, and aspiring managers, it simply doesn't make sense.

I firmly believe that in filling high-level positions, there must be a mutual understanding and agreement concerning what the person can do for the company and what the company can do for the person—right from the beginning.

I feel confident that executives and managers of tomorrow will be required to write their own performance descriptions prior to being hired. Why do I believe this? First, performance descriptions make good common sense. They help to establish goals, and they're an excellent communications tool. Most important is the fact that each person knows his or her own unique strengths, weaknesses, and capabilities, and these can be readily set forth in a performance description. Therefore, the performance description allows the decision maker to make "people decisions" on the basis of facts, not feelings or emotions. By putting together your own performance description, you're servicing yourself into a position (promoting and packaging yourself), which is a logical continuation of your efforts so far.

Performance description defined

A performance description is the interpretation of a position prepared by the person holding it or aspiring to hold it. It establishes, in detail, the following aspects of a position:
1. The benefits to be derived
2. The duties and responsibilities (functions)
3. The knowledge, skill, and experience requirements
4. The personality requirements
5. The follow-up requirements

In doing this, the performance description also defines:
1. The extent and nature of the authority
2. The methods and tools that are used
3. The accountability factors

Your own performance description should do the following:
1. Attract attention and interest
2. Communicate and support the benefits you have to offer
3. Communicate the benefits you specifically can provide to the industry and the company and to the position of your choosing
4. Reinforce your previous efforts
5. Sell

In short, then, this is an action plan of organization, a communications tool used to assist in the identification and development of your potential to effectively contribute in the position of your choosing.

Do they really want a water-walker?

There is frequently a substantial difference between what decision makers truly want (and hire) and what they "think" they want (and hire).

As to product

How often have you gone shopping for one thing, only to come home with something entirely different? Perhaps you bought an item because it met part of your needs or because it solved some other problem that you suddenly realized you had. Now relate this to your job-hunting efforts. The fact that you're there with the decision maker—that your attitude, ability, and character all seem to be right—is important.

However, sometimes we want to be told what we need. For example, when you go to your doctor, he'll give you a careful examination and ask a number of questions. Then, he'll call upon his experience and knowledge to tell him what your problem is, and possibly he will prescribe a medication. That's what you went there for—something to solve your problem. Your performance description can be likened to a prescription, except that it is *your* game plan. You're telling the decision maker how you might assist in solving any future problems, and you're helping the decision maker to see what he or she really needs.

It's important that you put your "prescription" in writing, just as the doctor does. It's easy to talk and to make promises, but putting something in writing takes effort and confidence—the confidence that says, "I *can* do what you need done. I *am* the person you want and need."

As to price

How often have you spent more on an item than you intended to? Although the price was high, you made the purchase because of the high quality of this product or service. You may have said to yourself, "It doesn't cost that much more to go first class, but the difference is well worth it."

In this chapter, you'll concentrate on showing decision makers that you're well worth the cost of their going first class.

"I did it my way"

Writing your performance description will help you interpret the position as you view it, in your own way. It will increase your knowledge not only of the position as it is outlined in the job description but also of the position as it *could be* if it were delivered into your hands. Your performance description effectively assists you in establishing and communicating *goals,* not only those associated with this position, but also your professional goals and the way these will benefit you, the decision maker, and the company.

A sample performance description is presented in Appendix B. However, each position has a unique set of ingredients. Accordingly, you must customize the job descriptions you've acquired at the initial interviews in such a way that they will reflect your own capabilities, interests, and aspirations.

If the company doesn't have a job description available, it's up to you to make one and then follow up with it. As a guide, use the performance description in Appendix B, or one of the other job descriptions you've acquired during your other interviews, or you can consult one of the many available books on job descriptions. Don't worry if your first or second effort isn't perfect. You'll be amazed at how good a writer you can be if you just keep at it.

"But I'm not a literary genius"

"Hell," you say, "I'm not a writer. I'm a sales manager [or a plant manager or whatever]." Well, I'm not a writer either, and believe me, if I can do it, anyone can. Until not so long ago, the thought of writing a book never occurred to me, but here it is—because it was needed.

Anything is possible—if you'll only try

Any excuses you can come up with are beside the point. You, as an aspiring executive or manager, must be capable of communicating. If you can't speak and write, you shouldn't be in such a position. Furthermore, writing your performance description will give you practice in writing about your favorite subject—"you" and your ability to successfully function and contribute.

It will be a pleasant, creative exercise, and you'll be surprised at some of the excellent information you'll be able to generate. This written communications tool (game plan) will enable you to become even more aware of the needs, problems, goals, and various functions associated with your position-to-be.

"Where do I start?"

Again, as you were told in Chapter 3, don't let any negative thoughts enter your mind. The most difficult thing about this whole exercise is getting started—so do it! Once you've started, ideas will flow. Here's how it's done:

1. The purpose of combining the person description and the job description is to enable you to identify problems and outline their possible solutions. Having done this, you should introduce personality requirements, giving your views on the characteristics and traits that would best qualify a person to solve these prob-

lems. Make it *your* performance description by pointing out that you have these characteristics and traits.

2. Then picture yourself in your niche. As you do this, write about your goals in this position and about what you would like and dislike about it.

3. Next review the major problems faced by the industry and the specific company as well as those you would encounter, should you be hired for this position. Record all this information.

4.. Review the section entitled Hints on Preparation in Chapter 9.

5. Determine the specific problems you can do something about.

6. Take seven sheets of paper and label each one as follows:
   a. Introduction
   b. Benefits to be derived
   c. Duties and responsibilities
   d. Knowledge, skill, and experience requirements
   e. Follow-up requirements
   f. Personality requirements
   g. Closing

7. Choose a function which you've identified as being of major importance, such as the sales function. Identify the benefits you can provide in this area. Then move to the next sheet and write down the duties and responsibilities, and so on. As you work, some excellent thoughts for the introduction should occur to you.

8. Ask yourself, "Do I really answer the questions of 'what,' 'where,' 'why,' and 'how'? In doing so, do I prove that the 'who'—the best person for that position—is me?"

9. Then move on to the next function and identify it. Have a separate set of papers for each function. You'll find that your comments will be repeated in some instances. In others, there will be a large number of responsibilities and duties, which may mean that you're dealing with several functions. You must then separate them and identify them individually.

10. Follow each major area for contribution through the steps outlined to its logical conclusion. Remember that many of these functions will overlap. This is good because it will show your potential employer your synergistic abilities and capacities.

11. Now edit out all the unnecessary information to a point where you feel you have a reasonable, succinct, and demonstrative performance description. Yes, you'll be doing a lot more work than just copying or adapting a job description. But your effort will prepare you to give in-depth answers to any question that might be thrown at you.

Definitions

Introduction

The introduction is meant to call the decision maker's attention (to bring forward for his or her consideration) your potential to contribute and to solve problems. It is a direct and to-the-point selling section.

Benefits to be derived

For each of the major functions to which you can contribute, specifically identify the positive results to be derived as a result of your efforts.

Duties and responsibilities

These are the actions required of you—what you will feel bound (obligated) to do in this specific position (and in these identified functions). These also include the efforts for which you will be accountable—the functions under your control.

Knowledge, skill, and experience requirements

These are the qualities or performable abilities required of you in accordance with the duties and responsibilities you've identified. They include:
1. Your acquaintance with information, facts, truths, and/or principles gained through your study and investigation
2. Your ability to perform as a result of your having acquired knowledge firsthand and put it into practice
3. The practical wisdom you have acquired regarding an identified function

Follow-up requirements

These are the acts required to ensure and reinforce the effectiveness of your efforts.

Personality requirements

These are the distinctive and perhaps unique and notable qualities or characteristics which you possess and which constitute your personality—the type of personality you feel one should have to accomplish the goals of this position.

Closing

The closing should be a simple sentence or paragraph summing up the preceding sections.

"Just how long should this be?"

How long your performance description should be depends entirely on the depth of your knowledge, abilities, and your target. There is a logical relationship between what you aspire to and the effort required. A newly selected manager might have a relatively simple two- to four-page performance description for one position and an eight- to fourteen-page one for another. However, someone who aspires to be the president of a major corporation might have a very involved and lengthy performance description.

In your dealings with decision makers, you might find that an effort such as this isn't extensive enough and that additional information is required, especially if you're introducing a new concept or program—creating that position. However, if you find during your interviewing that you communicate well with the decision maker and that your efforts will be quite similar to those outlined in the job description, you might choose simply to personalize this job description and expand on specific areas in a brief manner. Again, it is important to mention areas in which you can make unique contributions.

"What if I say something the decision maker doesn't like?"

At this point, you might well be worried about saying something wrong. Remember that nobody's perfect. No matter how hard you try, you can't always please everyone.

You don't want to work where your capabilities and talents will go unappreciated or be put to little use, do you? It's best to have a good understanding, on both sides, right from the start. This way, both you and your employer will avoid mistakes and assumptions. Your niche and its foundations must be secure and strong from the day you begin work.

Your performance description will also enable you and the decision maker to communicate effectively as needs and requirements change. If not enough attention is being paid to one specific function, he or she can call your attention to this and allow you to concentrate more of your efforts there.

Perhaps a function will need to be eliminated, expanded, or added. Again, your superior can ask you what you feel should be done, and you can incorporate your ideas into your performance description for review and approval.

A "pumpkin," you say

No, this whole effort hasn't suddenly turned into a pumpkin. Becoming a successful executive isn't easy. If it were, you wouldn't be reading this book. Once you start your performance description and begin to recognize its value, the necessary motivation, interest, and enthusiasm will start to come from within you. So go to it! Don't allow your efforts to turn into a pumpkin. It's not midnight, no matter how young or old you are. It's never too late to be what you can be.

Some final reasons for making this effort

Finally, giving your employer-to-be a listing of your major strengths and allowing that person to decide where and how to channel your efforts will enable you to utilize your talents fully and to enjoy them as well.

Additionally, your performance description will enable a potential employer to make an intelligent appraisal of you as a professional on the basis of your projected ability to perform—not on the basis of personality, race, creed, sex, age, or anything else. It will afford the decision maker the opportunity to assist you in carving your niche, and he or she will be able to take advantage of your identified skills, talents, and abilities and put them to their best use in the areas where there is the greatest need for them. If some of your capabilities are such that your superior or other executives can use them in areas currently handled improperly by another member of the staff, you'll be that much further entrenched in your niche.

Finally, if you accept a position for which you have set the goals, duties, and responsibilities, there can be no complaints or misunderstandings either on your part or on the part of management.

Let's remember that you're doing this for *yourself* with a specific company or group of companies in mind. If you make this effort and get turned down, it's on to newer and better things.

Packaging

You should make your performance description as presentable and attractive as possible. You'll be preparing only about five of them, so why not go first class—perhaps even have them permanently bound? Your performance description is valuable and useful and very much worth the decision maker's serious consideration; make it look that way.

You might introduce color, pictures, or graphs, for example, to make your performance description more interesting and informative. Use your imagination, but remember to keep it professional.

A critical appraisal

After you have finished your performance description and have had your "mentor" review it, show it to a management professional whose opinion you respect. Say that you want an honest opinion and some assistance in editing. This person's ideas and insights can prove invaluable.

Your follow-up to the performance description

The purpose of your follow-up is to determine whether your marketing effort is right. This means going back to the decision maker to find out what the results of your combined efforts have been. This will enable you to take the final action regarding your potential position—that niche. You'll receive either a "yes" or a "no." Either you'll have a great chance of being hired, or you'll be turned down.

Your chances for success are tremendous if:
1. You've listened carefully to the targeted decision makers.
2. You've gotten all their messages, determined their needs, and pressed their "hot buttons."
3. You've faithfully done all the things you've been told to do.

Two other considerations are also of importance, of course—your references and your income requirements. These are the subjects of the next two chapters.

If the answer is "no"

If the answer is "no," it's on to the next potential employer. Even so, you can feel confident that your efforts were the best and most knowledgeable of which you were capable. If you have been in touch with three to five companies, the chances are good that success is within your grasp.

Yes, you'll get tired, frustrated, and disappointed. You'll ask,

"Why is this taking so long? Don't they appreciate me and every thing I can do for them?" Here's a promise: Once the gates open, job offers will start to flow in. They might not come immediately—tomorrow or the next day—but you'll receive them, and what an ego-boosting experience it will be! You should continue your efforts until you have at least three meaningful job offers—in writing.

THIRTEEN

References and Recommendations

The other day, in a restaurant, I couldn't help overhearing a man say: "I'd been wanting to tell my boss off for years—tell him what I really thought of him and what an idiot he was. Finally I decided to quit, and on my last day I went in and gave it to him with both barrels. It made me feel so good."

At first, you can't help but identify with this man. However, what is his statement really telling you about him as a professional—as a gentleman?

Well, it's saying he's stupid—stupid for staying in a position where he hated his boss for years. Next, it's saying he can't communicate. Perhaps if he'd communicated over the years with his former boss, he could have helped his boss, himself, and the company. Maybe he could have saved the company tremendous amounts of time, effort, and money and grown a lot himself while doing this. Think of how much anguish, disappointment, and frustration he might have been spared. Maybe he could have developed a tremendous relationship with his boss built on mutual respect for each other's abilities, skills, and talents. They might have grown successfully as a team. Finally, his statement is saying that he's not thinking ahead—about what this tirade will mean to his future.

References, especially those from your former employer or

employers, are an extremely important ingredient in your search efforts. If you leave an employer with a poor record and a history of problems and negatives, then you might well end up recalling that quotation about reaping what you sow.

Remember that it doesn't take too many negative opinions of you on the part of a former employer to turn off an employer-to-be. This person's selection responsibility includes projecting you into the position—projecting your good points as well as your not-so-good ones. If he or she hears enough bad things about you—well, you can figure it out for yourself.

Reference defined

A reference is a source of information regarding one's character, attitudes, abilities, and past performance. To a potential employer, the most important and credible reference source is your former employer. Next in importance are people who have known you in a professional capacity.

References from your minister, priest, former schoolteachers, neighbors, and acquaintances are generally considered to be without much value. Top executives who know you can add credibility to your efforts and can be used effectively in some instances. We shall cover this later.

Here are some commandments regarding references: *Thou shalt always leave an employer with good feelings toward you—you'll need them someday; Thou shalt provide the names of reference sources only when there is a definite and expressed interest;* and *Thou shalt speak only positively of a former employer.*

Knowledgeable decision makers will *personally* do reference checking, and they will ask a lot of questions about you, both professionally and personally. They'll ask about your positives and your negatives. Remember that they don't want to make a mistake. Look at the sample reference check sheet shown in Figure 5. If you were thinking of hiring someone whose former employer answered "no" to some of these questions and hedged on others, maybe you'd say to yourself, "Dammit, I've got enough problems now without hiring some more."

Mending bridges

"But," you say, "I've had problems in the past." OK, everyone is entitled to a few mistakes. After all, you're human. But remember that life is short and negative memories are long.

REFERENCE CHECK SHEET

Name of candidate: _____ Date: _____

Former employer (reference): _____

Name: _____ Title: _____ Phone: _____

Address: _____ City: _____ State: _____ Zip: ____

We wish to verify some statements given us by _____ ,
who has given you as a reference. We would appreciate your help with the following questions.
Please be advised that any information provided will be held in the strictest of confidence.

1. Dates of employment: From: _____ To: _____
2. What position(s) did he(she) hold while in your employ? _____
   _____ Number of employees supervised? _____
3. What major functions did he(she) perform? _____
   _____
4. Could you tell me something about his(her) salary? _____
   bonus? _____ commission? _____ profit sharing? _____
5. Did he(she) have any responsibility for management decisions or policy formulation?
   _____ How much? _____ Comments: _____
6. What single word would you use to describe his(her):
   a. Attitude: _____   *c*. Ability: _____
   b. Appearance: _____   *d*. Character: _____
7. Does he(she):
   a. Accept responsibility?   ____   *i*. Demonstrate initiative?   ____
   b. Drink?   ____   *j*. Have financial problems?   ____
   c. Gamble?   ____   *k*. Seem industrious?   ____
   d. Use drugs?   ____   *l*. Seem to be liked by: Peers?   ____
   e. Have domestic problems?   ____   Superiors?   ____
   f. Appear creative?   ____   Those served? ____
   g. Respect established policy? ____ *m*. Accept constructive criticism? ____
   h. Think independently?   ____
8. Does he(she) exhibit regular attendance and willingness to vary schedule to meet employer
   needs? _____ Complete assignments? _____
9. Reason, and circumstances, for leaving? _____
10. Would you rehire? _____ Comments: _____

Thank you for your assistance.

Name: _____

Title: _____

Fig. 5

If you've made a mistake with your former boss, invite him or her to lunch or cocktails and mend those bridges. This could mean the difference between success and failure. If you and your former boss patch up your differences, you might even ask for a letter of recommendation. It surely won't hurt to try. So what if you have to eat crow or go with hat in hand? And remember that the anticipation is always worse than the realization. You just might be pleasantly surprised to find that time has healed all wounds.

A right—and a responsibility

Any boss has the right to fire anybody on the staff who doesn't belong to a union. If you've been fired, you probably don't have a leg to stand on. Like it or not, the boss has the last word.

Ask your former boss whether you might possibly receive a good reference. If you're unable to reach that former boss by phone, write a concerned letter asking permission to use his or her name and saying that you'll be calling shortly. Then do it.

Written references

When you're about to resign or be terminated, you should ask for a letter of recommendation (not a reference). Positive memories can be all too short. After you leave, problems invariably arise, and you won't be there to solve them. Possibly you will be blamed for your boss's errors or those of others in the department. Suddenly, you go from good guy to bad guy. Then, in answer to a question about you, your former boss might say, "Yes, I honestly thought he was an excellent employee and was disappointed when he resigned. However. . . ." Then come the comments and innuendos.

If something like this should occur and you have a very good letter of recommendation, you can counter with, "All right, if I was so bad, why did they keep me around for five years and give me those raises and promotions?" or "They didn't *have* to give me that letter of recommendation. Now that I'm gone, possibly they're realizing just how much I *did* contribute. You can believe what you want to, but I've got this in *writing*—backing up my position."

Other letters

Letters of recommendation might come from executives and others outside the company as well. In short, when you've done something well and have been commended for it, why not ask that this be put in writing? For the most part, people will be happy to oblige.

If you're being terminated

It's better to do things right, no matter what the circumstances. If you're going to be laid off or terminated or if you plan to quit, do everything possible to leave with a good name and record. When "your time" comes, remember that no one wants to hurt anyone else. Accept the inevitable as a professional. Here's an example of how you might handle the matter:

> "You've been very fine in affording me this opportunity. For the most part, I've tried to do my best. I'm very sorry things didn't work out, but maybe it's best for both of us. Can I count on you for a good recommendation? It's a pretty lonely world out there, and I'll be pounding on doors. I'd really appreciate all the help you can give me in the form of a good recommendation in writing."

Once you learn the boss's side of the story, start mending bridges. Don't argue or fight; agree with your manager. You want and need a good recommendation. Don't blame anybody for anything. You need goodwill now, not ill feelings. Get the boss on your side and then ask for a letter of recommendation—*not* a letter of reference.

Let's discuss the difference between the two.

Letter of reference

> Mr. _____ worked at our company from _____ to _____. His position was that of _____. He was promoted from _____ to _____. He was terminated because of _____ in this department. We're sorry to see him go.

In short, a letter of reference says very little.

Letter of recommendation

> Miss _____ worked at our company from _____ to _____. She handled her position with our company very capably. She did _____. Additionally, she _____. She increased _____. Her talents and abilities will be greatly missed.

This is more of a performance evaluation.

Resigning gracefully

Remember that when you leave a company's employ, for whatever reason, your boss will be feeling a little guilty. He or she will see that you're hurting and will identify with you, perhaps thinking, "Thank God I'm the boss and this isn't happening to me." However, remember a week or a month from now, the boss won't be feeling this way.

Say to your boss:

"Quite frankly, I need this letter of recommendation to get another position. I understand why you're doing this, and I know it has to be done. If I were in your shoes, I'd do the same thing. I agree that I didn't do _____, but I did contribute quite a bit in _____. I would sincerely appreciate a *good* letter of recommendation. Would you be so kind?"

Moving to a competitor

Here are some examples of how to handle this effectively.

"I have mixed emotions about this, but I've been solicited by another company. They've offered me an outstanding opportunity. After a great deal of soul-searching, I've decided to accept the offer. Now, before you say anything, I want you to know how much I've appreciated the opportunities you've afforded me. It's been just great. If it hadn't been for you and this company, I would never have been solicited, and I'd never be able to command the kind of income they're offering, so *thank you very much.* Our relationship has been great. I'm going to miss you, this department, and all these fine people, but this opportunity is too darned good. I just can't turn this one down."[1]

At this point, your boss will want to have his or her say. Listen carefully and courteously and then close with the following:

"Thanks for understanding. Oh yes, one other matter. Can you do me a favor? I'd sincerely appreciate your giving me a letter of recommendation. I know I've got this other position, but *if* it's necessary for the next one down the road, I'd really appreciate having it."

And there *will* be another position. When this company has benefited you all it can and when you've given it all you wish to give it, then move on—where you can grow faster and contribute more. Get those letters of recommendation. For all you know, that boss could drop dead, move several times, or become impossible to locate, or you could end up being blamed for things that went wrong after you left. Then what will you or your potential employer do? This way, you'll have something with which to protect yourself. How about the following?

"Incidentally, I'd really appreciate a performance review. By the way, what are you going to say about me? Can I count on you for a good review? It's very important to me and to my future. The

[1]Of course, here you're setting yourself up for a very nice counteroffer, which we'll discuss in the next chapter.

position I'm going to is a good one, and I'm sure they'll be calling you for a reference. Anything you can do to help will sincerely be appreciated."

The ifs and whens of reference checking

Will your employer-to-be check your references? Probably not, although no one can ever say for sure. But it's best to be safe. I've learned more about some candidates during a ten-minute conversation with their former employers than I could have found out during months of reference checking. If there are problems in your background and you haven't been able to straighten things out with your former employer, lay it on the line to your employer-to-be. Tell your side of the story—*before* your potential employer hears the bad news from someone else and *after* he or she has been sold on you. Do this at the second or third interview—one of the formal interviews—and don't belabor the point.

First find out whether your employer-to-be intends to check your references. For example:

"Incidentally, will you be doing any reference checking?" [The interviewer will probably say "yes" whether this is true or not.]

or

"How far do you usually go back?"

or

"Would you like *me* to give you the names or present locations of my former superiors?"

Regarding a previous employer with whom you had trouble, you might say:

"If you are, I just wanted you to know that you might have a little difficulty with one of my former employers. You'll probably have to go through the personnel department, and you'll have to have a written letter of authorization from me for the release of any information. Even then, they probably won't tell you much. [Here's where those letters will come in handy.] However, I have a letter of recommendation from my former superior."

This will probably satisfy your employer-to-be, who will then drop the subject, thinking that it's too much trouble to do all that checking and write all those letters. However, if he or she really wants to delve into the gory details, you might come up with a comment such as:

> "You know that I left that company. I had made a mistake—I'm only human. I'm thankful for the opportunities they provided while I was there, but it turned out to be best that I leave. I've since gone on to newer and greater endeavors and look forward to doing a fine job with you and your company. I want you to know that I'm happy you're asking all these questions and showing this concern. If you weren't, I'd be worried. Now could we get back to [some of your accomplishments] that we were talking about?"

In short, play it as close to your chest as possible, but be honest!

Remember that reference checks are used to confirm or disconfirm a decision maker's positive and/or negative feelings about you. A decision maker won't ask for references unless he or she is very interested in you. These checks may be done either before or after you've been hired. Accept them.

Many companies and managers consider reference checking to be poking their noses into places where they don't belong. However, if *you* were going to hire someone, wouldn't you want all the information you could get to assist you in making the right decision? So put yourself in your potential employer's shoes. Who knows more about your ability to perform than your former boss?

Forewarned is forearmed

Situation 1: You're getting nowhere. Your former boss is somehow too busy to talk to you and doesn't return your calls.

Situation 2: You thought you had this job in your pocket. In fact, you had even started to celebrate. Then suddenly, it was all off.

Situation 3: That S.O.B. you used to work for was incredibly two-faced. You really never knew where you stood with him, and to this day you still don't.

Suggested methods of handling these situations

If you've tried everything as outlined above and still are getting nowhere, have a *close* friend call your former employer on the phone and do a reference check. This friend must be a legitimate decision maker in a real company. The reasons for this will be obvious to most readers, but for those of you who are new to the game, many employers protect themselves by using ploys such as:

1. Providing information in writing only. For example, they require the person doing the checking to send a letter, to which they will respond.
2. Asking the name, title, and phone number of the person doing the checking. Then they phone back and discreetly ask questions before speaking with that person.

If your close friend ascertains that you got a poor reference, it's time to tell the truth again. Go to your potential employer and try something like this:

> "Listen, I've had some problems with my former employer. [Explain the situation, but don't put anyone in a bad light.] We had a personality problem. She didn't like me, and I didn't like her, and that's the reason I'm sitting in this chair. I'd rather not go into more detail. She is an awfully nice person; she's very competent and does an excellent job with that company. It's just that we didn't get along, and you can expect a poor reference."

Handling applications if you've been terminated

If you were terminated, the following are all good to use on an application form as reasons for having left a former employer:

Personality conflict
Communications problem
Differences over policy, resulting in resignation

Common courtesy

Whenever you use anyone's name as a reference, it is only courteous to ask his or her permission in advance. If you're going to use the name of someone other than your former employer as your reference, write to ask for permission and say that you'll be calling to make sure that it's all right. Ask this person to tell the truth about you and your performance. At the end of the conversation or letter, express your thanks for this assistance. You might even request a copy of any correspondence sent or received in this regard.

To cover every base, you might even call the person whom you are using as a reference again before giving his or her name to a potential employer. Say that so-and-so of such-and-such company will be calling regarding you and that you want to say "thank you" again for the reference.

The shoehorn approach

Throughout this book, I've tried to point out the importance of service—*your* service and attention to detail. You're trying to carve a niche for yourself, and this involves making it easy for that chosen employer to hire you. *Service yourself this position.*

Take much of the effort out of reference checking. As you've seen, this is another difficult task which a prospective employer must perform. He or she has to figure out which questions to ask, contact your references (perhaps calling each one three or more times before getting through), write letters, get your OK (in writing), etc.

After you've decided on the right position—the single most desirable one—you can use the shoehorn approach effectively. This approach has so many good and important features that I find it difficult to understand why it's not used more frequently. It says so much about you, your follow-up, your abilities, and finally your interest in the position. It also guarantees an excellent recommendation and reemphasizes your uniqueness.

How it works

Recognizing that decision makers are very busy, that problems out of sight are problems out of mind, and that recall works best if aided properly, continue your campaign on all levels:

1. Line up people—former bosses or other top executives in your former company or other companies—who know you on a professional level.
2. Advise each of them of the position you're seeking with the one company you've selected. If possible, meet with them personally and show each your profile and/or your performance description.
3. Tell these people that you need their assistance in the form of a recommendation and that your acquiring this position might very possibly hinge on what they're going to say about you.
4. Give them the name, phone number, and title of the decision maker (possibly they'll need the address as well). Ask each one to call (or write) in your behalf, outlining your assets, abilities, and skills (gleaned from your profile) and asking whether there are any additional insights regarding you that they might be able to provide.

This approach should serve to convince the decision maker that you are, indeed, the right person for the position—that it is your niche.

Finally

Once you're in that position, it is only common courtesy to again contact people who helped in your efforts. Write thank-you letters. Don't forget your former employer when it comes to thank-you letters and follow-up, whether you parted on friendly terms or not.

Exit letter

When you leave, do it with style. Show your style and prove that you are a professional. Write a real thank-you letter, such as the following:

> Dear _____:
>   I wanted to take this opportunity to say a warm and sincere "thank you" for the opportunities you've afforded me during the last _____ years.
>   This experience has made me a lot more knowledgeable and capable in the _____ industry. I look forward with great anticipation to using many of the skills I've learned while in your employ.
>   To show my appreciation, I'd like to suggest some things that might help you and the company in the future. [Your comments here must be concerned only with reinforcing positive aspects; this is *not* poison-pen time.]
>   I sincerely trust that you will accept these ideas in the spirit in which they are offered, and I look forward to maintaining our relationship in a positive manner over the years.
>   Sincerely,

The left hook

What do you do when your boss says, "Write a letter of recommendation and say what you feel is necessary—I'll sign it"? He or she is saying this for several reasons:

1. It's hard to be objective when writing such a letter.
2. Writing a letter of recommendation takes valuable time.
3. The boss doubts that you'll take the time to write it yourself.

The only way to handle such a situation is to write the letter. Type it (or have it typed) neatly on company stationery and give it to your boss. Ask for his or her approval and for suggestions concerning additions or deletions. The following is an example of such a letter of recommendation:

> XYZ Company
> To whom it may concern:
> The following are examples of correspondence received by our company "unsolicited" as a result of the efforts of _____ :
> [Excerpt] _____
>
> _____[Company name, Name, Title]
> [Excerpt] _____
>
> _____[Company name, Name, Title]
> Since 19— she has contributed on a continuing basis to the growth and ongoing successes of our company.
> Here are some contributions she has made:
> 1. Saved our company _____
> 2. Created a _____
> 3. Was responsible for _____
> 4. Directed the activities of _____
> 5. _____

It is with mixed emotions that I accept her resignation from our company because I realize that keeping her here would limit her potential. She has been an outstanding, exceptional employee. She will be greatly missed.

I feel certain that any company which is successful enough to acquire her talents will be fortunate indeed.
Sincerely,

FOURTEEN

Negotiation

What's wrong with driving a Mercedes Benz, a Cadillac Seville, a BMW, a Lincoln Continental, or even a Rolls-Royce? How about living in a finer home, buying a vacation home, and having extra funds for the nicer things in life—perhaps a country-club membership or private schooling for the kids? In short, why not have all those things that really successful people seem to have? You *can* have them—or at least some of them—if you find that niche and *are paid in relation to your contributions to the company and the position of your choosing.*

If other people can have these things, why can't you? Just make up your mind and think positively. *Then work to make it happen!*

We're talking about money, the first time we've discussed it in this book. So far we've talked about everything but money. But now we've got to get down to the nitty-gritty—the "bottom line."

When you go out to buy a car or a home, for example, you have to pay for it with money. On completion of the sale, you're given a contract or receipt. The rules of negotiation require that salespeople sell their products for the best price they can get. Buyers, on the other hand, must negotiate for the lowest price. Unless you think you're worth a lot, how do you expect the decision maker to value your services? Think rich! Act rich! Keep on referring back to your established goals. Add new ones and then work constantly to achieve them.

Negotiation concerns

If you consider that you have management potential or abilities, you must learn the art and skills of negotiation. As in love and war, there are times in negotiation when no holds are barred. Negotiation is business—a straightforward exchange between concerned parties during which price, value, or worth is mutually agreed upon.

Negotiation of compensation—your compensation—is the culmination of all your efforts. In this endeavor you must be fully prepared, anticipate all problems, and, most important, move positively, carefully, and methodically during the session, leaving nothing to chance or misunderstanding. Errors in communication can cause ulcers, disappointments, and terminations, among other things. As you do the exercises set forth in this chapter, you must decide which matters are of greatest importance to you. Make up a checklist and take it with you to your negotiating session so that you will be sure to cover everything properly and completely. Refer to it during your session. You might well practice negotiating with your mentor.

Some of the most common problems encountered during a negotiating session are the following:
1. Making assumptions
2. Being unwilling to consider or introduce alternatives
3. Not listening carefully
4. Failing to ask the right questions
5. Not communicating—not "telling it like it is"
6. Letting the emotions rule
7. Failing to recap the understanding
8. Not getting the agreement in writing
9. Not concentrating on short-term considerations as well as long-term ones

Before the session

Your income *must be negotiated before you accept any position.* Don't be overly anxious to jump at a first offer. Furthermore, no employer expects you to accept a first offer—immediately. If you do, you'll appear to be either desperate or very inexperienced.

As I've said all along, in your search efforts you must strive for at least three job offers. This will enable you to bargain from a position of strength. Of course, being currently employed gives you even greater strength.

Finally, if you seem willing to accept an offer before it is even made, the decision maker may well take this opportunity to snatch up a bargain and offer you the "rock bottom." Remember that decision makers have the responsibility to get you for the best price possible.

When does the negotiating begin?

You've gone through a number of follow-up interviews. How will you know when you've succeeded—made the sale? How will you know when you've been invited to step into your niche? How will you know when to stop selling and take the order?

You'll know by the signals the decision maker is sending out. Here are some examples:

1. "You'll be doing this, this, and this. . . ."
2. "When you join our company, you will be. . . ."
3. Long, in-depth interviews.
4. A good feeling that you like each other.
5. "When can you start?"
6. "How much notice do you have to give?"
7. "What will it take to bring you on board?"
8. "I want you to meet Mrs. _____ ,who will be helping you learn the ropes."
9. "We want you to go into the field with one of our salespeople and see, firsthand, what the position is like and what you'll be doing."
10. "I want you to go to lunch with one of our people who went through our training program about ten months ago and has done very well. She'll be able to tell you a lot about our program and will be evaluating you as well."

A second interview tells you that you're on the way. A third interview tells you that you've made the sale and that now the decision maker just wants to be sure.

Contracts and letters of understanding

Letters of understanding (agreement) and contracts are the right way to enter into any business agreement. These must include not only the position title, the starting salary, and the duties and responsibilities of the position but also your understanding as to frequency of review (annually or, preferably, semiannually,) and other conditions of employment (to be explained shortly).

No matter what kind of business agreement or sale you are a party to, you should be offered a contract or a receipt. This is meant for the protection of all parties concerned. So how can you enter into an employment agreement (perhaps one of the most important understandings in your life) on the basis of a simple word-of-mouth understanding?

"But," you say, "they don't want to put this in writing." Well, this should make you suspicious immediately. Don't they believe in you? Don't they believe in themselves? Here's how you might handle such a situation:

> "Well, I've heard what you said. You know what you said. But six months from now, when it's time for that better car or that salary review, this letter will be a good reminder for us to get together again and talk about these matters—to review where we are and where we're going."

Professionally, I don't think any position is very worthwhile unless it offers a carrot—a carrot in the form of a bonus, a commission, or an incentive, in addition to salary.

Before we go any further, however, let's look at the things that can be considered part of your income (compensation package). This package can be broken down into two categories: (1) negotiable (presently or in the future) aspects and (2) nonnegotiable aspects.

Negotiable

1. Salary
2. Salary review
3. Bonus
4. Commissions
5. Company car or transportation allowance (in Europe, for spouse as well)
6. Expense-account reimbursement:
   a. Food
   b. Travel
   c. Lodging
   d. Miscellaneous
7. Club memberships
8. Stock options
9. Deferred compensation

    10. Severance pay
    11. Outplacement consulting
    12. Education allowances

Nonnegotiable

    1. Pension plan
    2. Profit sharing
    3. Vacations
    4. Sick leave
    5. Insurance programs:
        a. Medical
        b. Dental
        c. Life
        d. Disability
        e. Other
    6. Investment program (matching?)
    7. Other assistance:
        a. Loans (short-term)
        b. Financial planning
        c. Tax or CPA assistance
        d. Legal assistance

Remember that you and your employer must agree on all these things *before* you come on board. Remember too that the higher you move in a company's structure, the more perquisites ("perks") there are to be negotiated. For example, lower-level management people might be in a position to negotiate only salary, and even that will be within a fixed range. Bonuses and/or commissions are already set forth as company policy, as are the other negotiable elements. It is imperative that you have as many negotiable perks as possible defined in as much detail as you can. Some companies are incredibly picky about some of the most ridiculous things, and you must be likewise.

You owe it to yourself to be fully informed about these benefits. You are, in part, paying for them by your services in behalf of your employer. Make the most of every perquisite available.

Other factors

As to relocation

    1. Moving costs (to what maximum?)
    2. Travel for yourself and your spouse for real estate assessment
    3. Real estate brokerage costs

4. Interim expense reimbursement as for lodging, food, and transportation (and for how long)
5. Closing costs
6. Mortgage placement assistance
7. Guarantee as to company purchase of present home
8. Other incidentals

Bargain hunters everywhere?

Yes, you're good and you're worth a lot. In fact, you have the potential to make and/or save tremendous sums of money for a number of employers. Therefore, it's important that you carefully determine your value in relation to your needs—*both now and in the future.*

Before you start salary negotiations, you should carefully consider where you are financially and where you want to be. Here's another exercise concerned with goals.

Write the following on a piece of paper:

Amount needed monthly × 12   Amount wanted monthly × 12

House payment (rent)
Auto payment(s) (lease)
Home expenses:
    Heating
    Lighting
    Food
    Clothing
    Incidentals
    Entertainment
    Insurance
Anticipated expenses:
Expenses when planned goals are achieved:

Now add the additional things which you feel are necessary and important. Add as many considerations to this list as possible and make it as complete as you can. Then, just to be on the safe side of reality (taking today's inflation into account), add 15 to 20 percent to your figures.

All too many people have no idea of their worth, even in their present positions. For those who are unemployed—whose backs are against the wall and who are fending off the bill collector—"anything" is all right, and salary requirements are "open" or "negotiable." If you were a decision maker and sensed a bargain, wouldn't you take advantage of it? You must be very careful not to offer too much of a bargain or, at the other extreme, to price yourself out of the market. The only way to be sure is to ask questions and compare offers.

Salary first

Most companies will take your past salary history into account. If they really want you, they'll usually offer you more than you made in your last position. In making you an offer you can't refuse, a company will look at the three following things (among others, of course):

1. What you can mean in terms of dollars and cents to them
2. What their budget is
3. Your previous salary

Current practice says that a 15 to 20 percent *minimum* increase over present salary is necessary to attract an excellent talent. Perhaps as much as a 50 percent increase will be offered to attract a proved "winner." Remember, however, that you can't expect a 50 percent increase unless you can really offer a company something it desperately wants and needs. There's also the factor of *supply and demand*—don't forget your competition.

If you're not money-oriented or if you're hesitant about dealing with money matters, the above exercise will be helpful in that it requires you to base your price on a percentage—say, 15 to 25 percent over your estimated annual expenses.

Demand pricing

The above technique might have some merit, but modern marketing practice dictates that the "right price" for you must be based on your value to the company (your demand), not on your past salary history or on your cost of living plus a certain percent.

In this regard, if you really want an eye-opener, check into a book called *Dartnell's Annual Survey of Compensation*. This will really give you a lot of reason to be dissatisfied with your current income situation.

But, tell me, do you really think top executives figure their incomes on the basis of cost of living plus 20 percent? Would that really be thinking rich? No, top people don't think that way. Their companies pay them *very* well so that they won't have financial concerns. The incomes of top-management people are based on the demand for their *unique* talents and abilities. And the greater their monopolistic hold on unique talents and abilities, the stronger their niche and the higher incomes they can command.

The rules of the game

Let's look at the rules of the game:

1. Total compensation *must* be geared to performance.
2. You are more valuable if you are currently employed.
3. Go for the most money (head in the clouds and feet on the ground).
4. If the decision maker starts making promises, ask that these be tied to goals with commissions and/or bonuses which are achievable.
5. Don't rush into anything without sleeping on the offer.
6. Get the negotiations set forth in the form of a written contract or letter of understanding outlining the specifics. It's amazing how easily both you and your employer-to-be can forget things as time goes by. This is meant to protect you both.
7. Be sure to include basic understandings as to cost-of-living increases and merit raises—*as well as the frequency with which these are to be tendered.*
8. If you change positions, do so *only* if this means moving up the ladder financially and otherwise.

This brings up another matter. After doing so much work, you don't want to take the first thing that comes along unless you are absolutely positive that this opportunity is also the best opportunity. And so, another commandment: *Thou shalt always seek three or more offers and carefully compare them before accepting one.* If you use the methods you've learned in this book, you should readily be able to get several job offers—maybe even four or five. You must methodically compare them. The following exercise will help you do this.

Offer-comparison exercise

Make up a chart of all the negotiable and nonnegotiable elements to be considered in your compensation package. Number each one in relation to what you consider to be its relative importance. Then start another list of reasons for considering each position other than financial ones. Begin with the most important one and follow on through to the least important one. Now add each offer's combined elements together to determine the one with the smallest number. This will enable you to carefully and methodically compare the offers and to decide on the best all-around opportunity, avoiding concentration on salary or emotions alone.

Some sample offer-comparison charts are presented on the following pages. You can make up your own, adding or deleting elements to reflect your own concerns.

OFFER-COMPARISON CHART

FINANCIAL CONSIDERATIONS AND PERQUISITES

	COMPANY 1	COMPANY 2	COMPANY 3
1. Salary			
2. Salary review			
3. Bonus			
4. Commissions			
5. Company auto Transportation allowance			

6. Expense-account reimbursement:
  a. Food
  b. Travel
  c. Lodging
  d. Miscellaneous			

7. Club memberships			
8. Stock options			
9. Deferred compensation			
10. Severance pay			
11. Outplacement consulting			
12. Education allowances			
13. Pension plan			
14. Profit sharing			
15. Vacations			
16. Sick leave			

17. Insurance programs
  a. Medical
  b. Dental
  c. Life
  d. Disability
  e. Other			

18. Investment program (matching)			

19. Other assistance:
  a. Loans (short-term)
  b. Financial planning
  c. Tax or CPA assistance
  d. Legal assistance			

20. Moving expenses
  a. Travel expenses
  b. Lodging
  c. Food			

d. Transportation
e. Brokerage costs
f. Closing costs
g. Mortgage placement assistance
h. Guarantee as to home purchase
i. Incidentals

OFFER-COMPARISON CHART

CONSIDERATIONS OTHER THAN FINANCIAL ONES

	COMPANY 1	COMPANY 2	COMPANY 3
1. Opportunity and challenge			
2. Personality match			
3. Growth potential			
4. Product identification			
5. Company and industry identification			
6. Timing			
7. Boredom			
8. Upward mobility			
9. Growth pattern of company			
10. Growth pattern of industry			
11. Company location			
12. Position identification			
13. Relevancy to knowledge and experience			
14. Working conditions			
15. Your rating of the boss			
16. Soundness of the company			
17. Product obsolescence			
18. Relevance of marketing to company objective			
19. Gut feeling			
20. Feelings toward future coworkers			
21. Probability of fitting in			
22. Opportunity to be the person you really are, rather than putting on an act			
23. Probability of support from peers and superiors			
24. Relevance to long-term objectives			

Facts of life

Before we discuss the actual negotiating session, let's review some facts of corporate life:

1. Big dollars are found with big corporations in big cities.
2. The higher you go up the ladder, the fewer positions there are and the greater the competition.

3. Some companies and industries just don't pay good salaries.
4. The higher the security of a position, the lower the pay.
5. By creating a position for yourself, you put yourself way ahead of your competition—if you have any, that is.[1]
6. Matching your personality to that of your employer-to-be is an exceptionally important consideration.

A sample negotiating session

You've done all your homework. You have learned about salary levels and other perquisites associated with the position during your various interviews. The dialogue might go as follows:

> YOU: We've had a number of good meetings. I've told you my ideas about where I feel I might be able to contribute to this company. I feel I've given good reasons for wanting this position. My big question at this point is, do you want to hire me?
>
> DECISION MAKER: Well, we're quite impressed with _____ . However, we have some reservations about _____ .

This is called "intimidation." The decision maker is trying to undermine your confidence and your bargaining strength. Listen carefully. Write the objections down. After the decision maker has enumerated all his or her objections, ask whether there are any additional ones. Then challenge each objection, changing negatives to positives, and turning concerns and problems into opportunities for you and for the decision maker. You might even _turn the tables_. Once you've dealt with the decision maker's objections, say that you have some concerns as well and let the decision maker field these for you.

> YOU: I'm confident of my abilities to handle this position. Yes, I have a few negatives, but I'm sure you'll agree that the contributions I can make to this company and this position far outweigh any of these. Are you ready to make me an offer?

Then be quiet!

> DECISION MAKER: How much do you want?

[1]Why? Because there will be no set salary range, and the decision maker will be negotiating for your services on the basis of your potential to contribute, rather than working within some predefined range. This technique allows you to assist the decision maker in negotiating your base salary plus all the other perks which will be attractive to you both.

Early on, managers learn that a job hunter is harder on himself or herself than they could ever be. Accordingly, a favorite ploy is to throw the ball back in the lap of the job hunter (you). Remember that turnabout is fair play.

YOU: Well, that's up to you.

or

What do you consider to be a *good* offer?

DECISION MAKER: What do you mean, "That's up to me"? You must have some idea as to your cost of living, your expenses, and so on.

YOU: Yes, I do, but I never said I'd take this position on a cost-of-living basis or at a rock-bottom minimum. Are we talking about that? I thought we were talking about my contributing substantially in these areas: (1) _____ , (2) _____ , (3) _____ , (4) _____ , and (5) _____ . In other words, what am I worth to your company, both now and in the future? You've also told me what a fantastic company this is and how far ahead of its competitors it is. Let's keep talking at that level.

or

I consider myself a top-notch professional with top-notch qualifications who can command a top-notch salary. What am I worth to you? That's what we're really talking about, isn't it?

Here, again, you dump this in the decision maker's lap. You have a pretty good idea of the salary range, and you've set the decision maker up so that he or she is not going to insult you by offering you the bottom of that range. But remember one other very important factor: Listen carefully and don't become overly defensive during your negotiations. Don't show your anxiety by talking too much or appearing overly anxious. This *will* jeopardize your ability to bargain from a position of strength.

Silence can be a very effective tool if used properly. If you don't say anything in response to these leading questions, the decision maker will have to. And once he or she has made an offer, silence is again called for—no matter how good or bad the offer is. Then, if the offer is bad, say:

"Is this your best offer? Why?"

Whether it's an excellent offer or a terrible one, try this:

"I'd like to think about it for a couple of days and then get back to you. As you know from our earlier discussions, there are three companies I'm interested in. Of course, you're very high on the list.

However, I'd like to have a chance to compare their offers with yours. Incidentally, before we go any further, let's talk a little about tying my performance to a bonus or commission-type schedule, and could we put this in writing?"

Another commandment is needed at this point: *Thou shalt have every understanding regarding a position put in writing.* By not saying "yes" immediately, you are showing your business acumen and strength, and you won't have to regret your hasty decision if you get a much better offer the next day.

If you've jumped the gun

If you've jumped the gun, you can always go back to the first company and say, "I've just received a much higher offer. I honestly prefer your company and was wondering if you could possibly reconsider your offer?" Incidentally, if the person at the first company asks the name of the other one, it's none of his or her business.

Remember that companies have a lot more money and time than you do, and they know it. Waiting a few days won't hurt them. Furthermore, a company that is anxious to get your acceptance now might even "up the ante." In any case, the decision maker's reaction will tell you a great deal about his or her real interest in you and in having you join the company.

Here are some additional points for you to remember about negotiation:

1. Never lie about your income or about your educational achievements. These things are all too easy to check. You may be asked to bring in copies of your W-2 forms or your college transcripts.
2. Much of your salary potential will be based on your past income history.
3. *Your* responsibility is to go for the most that the position will pay.
4. The *company's* responsibility is to get you—the best person for the position.
5. You must establish realistic goals and stick with them.

In your salary negotiations, you must play the game. If you are about to get a raise or a cost-of-living increase in your present job or if you were about to in your former one, you must figure your salary at a higher figure, and you should mention this if asked. Remember that you've worked hard and deserve this.

Their side

Each company is going to make you what it considers to be a fair offer. If it's not acceptable to you, you must say so and give your reasons. For example:

> "Well, I'm now making $_____ , with an increase or review due soon. If I take this position, I'll be losing money. I don't find your offer substantial enough to warrant my making a change at this time."

or

> "I believe you're basing your offer solely on my current salary, and there are a lot of things you may not be taking into account, such as commissions, bonuses, and profit sharing. Most important, I've invested a lot of time and effort in this job. I've proved myself, demonstrated my abilities, and hired and trained my staff and my successor. In short, I've done everything a successful executive should do. My job is fairly secure. However, I feel like a fixture at my current employer, and I don't like that feeling. That's why I'm looking. But I do have security there. Can you offer me that?"

or

> "My total compensation package consists of _____. [Don't give a figure.] What is your total package?"

or

> "I have three offers from three different companies. I'm carefully considering your company, but, unfortunately, your offer is the lowest, and it isn't acceptable to me. But since I'm very interested in joining your company, let's renegotiate that starting salary."

If the offer is bad and the decision maker insists on an answer, this tells you one of three things:

1. You haven't told the decision maker everything that he or she should know about your total compensation package.
2. The decision maker is not realistic and is not fully sold on you.
3. You're sitting in the wrong place—get the heck out of there.

Positions with an established salary range

If you are going after a currently existing position, there will be an established salary range. For example, let's say that this is

$30,000 to $40,000—you've learned this during one of your follow-up interviews—and that you're making $28,000 now. Where do you start negotiating? At the top!

Always go for the top, but remember to throw the ball in the decision maker's lap. Make your counteroffer, and then the decision maker's offer will have to be related to yours. Then you can really get into some negotiating, as in the following example:

> DECISION MAKER: You're at $28,000 now, and I really can't talk about $40,000. I just couldn't get my boss to approve that.
>
> YOU: Well, when can I expect to be at that $40,000 level—six months, a year? That's part of the offer and is very important to me. Sure, I'll consider a lower counteroffer figure, but I'm going for the top figure because I *know* that I'm the best person for this position. Let's talk further and see what we can come up with, OK?

To be a good negotiator is to be respected

How can you expect to properly represent your employer-to-be if you can't even represent yourself? Proper negotiation requires that both parties bargain from positions of strength. If the negotiation is handled properly, you will be able to reach an understanding that makes you both happy. So if a counteroffer is realistic, go along with it.

Incidentally, in the example above, $33,000 to $35,000 would be the right offer for an above-average performer.

More insights

If you are dealing with the ultimate decision maker, he or she will be able to introduce some flexibility into the salary range. But if you're stuck with your immediate superior-to-be, here's something you should know. This person has been given the job of negotiation because the boss doesn't want it. He or she will be given a specific range within which to negotiate and will usually offer the lowest figure. To offer anything over that would require stringing you along.

However, this could be a blessing—the break of your lifetime. It might give you an opportunity to wait on those other offers (or make them happen) while they're busy stringing you along. Just keep on reminding yourself that *truly outstanding talent doesn't remain long in the marketplace.*

Next, in good companies with knowledgeable management, you won't be eligible for the company benefit programs for the first three months. This is the probationary period, during which you see whether the marriage will work. The end of the probationary period is an excellent time for both you and your employer to assess your future and—most important—your income in relation to that of others in the company in comparable positions.

"But I'm happy where I am—I'm just not making enough"

"They don't want to give me a raise," you say. Well, maybe you'd be happier elsewhere. If you're not appreciated—and I mean financially—by your present employer, then it's time to start looking carefully and very discreetly.

If and when you find a better niche, it's on to newer and greater opportunities, challenges, and happiness.

Counteroffers

Never accept a counteroffer from your present employer! "OK," your employer may say, "things will be different," "You'll get your raise—just hang in there a little longer," "Please bear with us: don't resign and take that other job," and so on. Well, hasn't this employer had enough time to appreciate you and show good faith?

Most employers will simply use a counteroffer to give them time to look for someone to replace you. And then, that's right—out the door.

"But I've decided that I really want this position"

Let's say that you really want a specific position, but the company doesn't want to pay your price. Remember, out of sight, out of mind. So let's do some more follow-up.

Write a nice, short, sweet, and to-the-point letter reaffirming your interest in the company and the position and pointing out the benefits you have to offer. Be sure to say that you're confident that you can do the job. Finally, say that you would like the company to reconsider its offer to you; otherwise, you might both suffer an injustice.

So you really want money—big money

If you're sure that the company is sold on you and if you're sure of yourself, the product, the company, and the industry, you might try a close like this:

> "I don't want a big salary, benefits, retirement, and so on. I want a nominal salary, say, $2,000, $3,000, or $5,000[2] a month—you know, so that I can afford those basics.
>
> "I'm confident of my abilities to sell and to get that job done. What I'm asking is for you to tie my performance (and that of my department) to an *open-ended* income structure and to do this in the form of a noncancelable contract so that we'll both be protected. I feel that 7 percent of the gross sales would be fair, don't you?
>
> This would give me a carrot, and you would get sales far beyond your expectations. That's what it's all about anyway, isn't it?"

[2]As determined by the exercise on p. 185.

FIFTEEN

Once You're There

What you get by reaching your destination is not nearly as important as what you become by reaching that destination.[1]

Great! You got what you consider to be "the position." Fantastic! Congratulations! It couldn't have happened to a finer person. Now's the time to continue on that road to success. The only way you can do this is with your follow-up—the continuing sale.

No book on job hunting would be complete without a chapter on holding onto a job once you have it. Most of the rules for getting a job are the same as those for holding it. You've invested a lot of time, effort, and money to make sure that you were right for the position and that it was right for you. Don't let anything hold you back now. Continue to make your success happen!

The successes, enthusiasm, and energy you're enjoying now, the energy that you never dreamed of having, have made your search, your efforts, worthwhile. I don't believe I've ever met anyone who regretted changing positions—if the change was a well-planned one. (I really don't need to add that, do I?) The one regret continually voiced is, "I only regret that I didn't do this sooner."

You should be aware of many of the reasons why things are

[1]John Hammond (ed.), *The Fine Art of Doing Better,* American Motivational Association, Los Angeles, 1974, p. 121. Author's royalties donated to Junior Achievement Inc.

going so well for you now. The newness of the position, the challenges, the opportunities, and your enthusiasm—all this is exciting, to say the least. Your new job should also give you the opportunity to express your own individuality in a way that somehow was never possible in your former positions.

Of course, you have to expect a little rough going at first. You're a stranger. Don't expect to be greeted as an old friend. You'll be held suspect until time and a lot of effort on your part confirm the company's initial impressions of you. Concentrate on doing what is required of you. Earn respect—don't demand it. One of the best ways of doing this is to listen carefully and ask for help— remember the magic sentence, "I need your help."

At the lower management levels, you must learn to be a good follower before you can lead. Once you've established a good track record and have gained respect, there'll be plenty of time to establish your own rules.

Things will change

As sure as there will be a tomorrow, things will change. Whether they change for the better or for the worse is mainly up to one person—you.

Keep referring to your action plan—your performance description. Keep your goals in mind; they are your blueprint for success. Remember the saying, "Plan your work, then work your plan."

There will always be opportunities, challenges, problems, in-fighting, politics, and competition from all directions. Remember to be prepared for change.

Don't think it can't happen to you

Here are a few things that can happen. All too often, I've heard of them happening to other people.

1. There is a management changeover right after you're hired.
   a. You can't stand your new boss.
   b. Your new boss can't stand you.
   c. Result: You're out.
2. You're in the middle of a training program. Things are going fantastically well, and you're learning and progressing.
   a. A policy decision is handed down. There will be no more

training programs. All new talent will come from the
competition.
  b. A small recession hits, profits are down, and manage-
     ment decides to cut the staff. All people who have been
     with the company less than a year are to be terminated.
  c. Result: You're out.
3. You begin in your new position.
  a. Your new boss expects a water-walker.
  b. Your new boss comes across differently from the way he
     or she did during those interviews.
  c. The people who interviewed you misrepresented:
     (1) The opportunity
     (2) The company's financial position
     (3) The position
  d. Result: You're out.

"I don't think that would ever happen to me," you say. (No one
ever does.) Well, believe me, all too many people who have found
themselves in situations like these have said exactly the same
thing.

Your quiet time

Set aside the first Tuesday night of each month. Tell your husband
or your wife that this is your night alone—no matter what.
(Maybe you'll need two nights a month—find out what's
best for you.) This is your night for positive self-reflection and
planning:
  1. Review the past month. Make a listing of the outstanding
     things you've accomplished, using your calendar and
     short-term listing of goals. Note a few accomplishments
     for each week. Concentrate on your successes and the
     reasons for these achievements.
  2. Ask yourself how these accomplishments are helping you
     to achieve your intermediate- and long-term goals.
  3. Determine how these accomplishments compare with the
     goals you established for yourself for the month.
  4. Establish goals for the coming month.
  5. Check your follow-up log.

After you do this, continue thinking good thoughts and enjoying the feeling of accomplishment. You should be refreshed and
ready to take on the new challenges that tomorrow will bring.
Remember that "the rich get richer thinking rich thoughts."

Define and recognize your best
friends (and your not-so-good-ones)

Your biggest stumbling blocks are *not* the people in your life who are grinding you down. They are:

1. Self-doubt
2. Anticipating the worst
3. Negative thoughts
4. Procrastination
5. Impatience
6. Excuses
7. Inaction
8. Lack of goals

In other words, don't get down on yourself. Remember that you are one of your own best friends, but you can also be your own worst enemy. The choice is yours.

Let's look at your ten best friends (besides your actual friends and your family, of course):

1. Knowledge
2. Love
3. Goals
4. Confidence
5. Enthusiasm
6. Energy
7. Quiet times
8. Play
9. Yourself, family, and friends
10. What this book is all about—your career

The end? No. For you, the beginning.

The Personal Profile

This appendix contains a sample professional profile. When sending your professional profile and performance description to a prospective employer, include a covering letter such as the following:

Don:

As you know, I've identified with the _____ industry and with the people in it for a number of years. The same characteristics of integrity, enthusiasm, initiative, and commitment which are shared by successful management in this industry are also important facets of my makeup.

By adding my knowledge, experience, and skills to the assets of your company and team (in New York), I feel that many successful synergistic results could be achieved.

My conversations with former and present WXYZ employees have assisted me in the identification of a number of problems currently faced by the company. I've got a tremendous number of ideas when it comes to solutions for these problems. (Please see my performance description.) However, I'm sure that your company—"the experts"—can teach me a lot of additional things.

Being very enthusiastic about WXYZ's future and its potential and feeling the same about myself, I sincerely look forward to exploring the possibilities of how our talents might be conjoined.

Respectfully submitted,

Robert G. Traxel

PROFESSIONAL PROFILE

PREPARED FOR: Mr. Donald Jamieson
WXYZ Products, Inc.
6390 W. Foothill Blvd.
New York, New York 10203

PREPARED BY: Robert G. Traxel

PHONE: 714-000-0000

DATE: January 27, 1976

Résumés, for the most part, are concerned with past experience and contributions made to former employers. Consequently, it is necessary for the reviewer to try to take this past experience and project it into the future and in this way determine the potentials of a candidate.

After spending nearly four years poring over résumés, all of which say relatively the same thing, I feel that the last thing I want to do is to present myself in such a manner. Accordingly, I have tried to present the positives and negatives about myself in a unique way that I hope will assist you in getting to know me professionally.

In the following self-analysis, I have covered four major categories: skills, goals, qualifications, and experience. These categories have been further broken down into general and specific subdivisions.

Once you have had a chance to review this material and the supporting documentation, I feel you will be able to make a critical appraisal of my potential to contribute to your organization.

SKILLS AND ABILITIES

GENERALIZED SKILLS

RELATING TO PEOPLE:
Skilled at mentoring, negotiating, supervising, consulting, instructing, coaching, persuading, diverting, exchanging information, taking instructions, helping, and serving

RELATING TO DATA:
Skilled at coordinating, innovating, analyzing, computing, and compiling, as well as assimilating and resolving complex relationships of data handling

RELATING TO THINGS:
Skilled mechanically, with a great ability to resolve intricate puzzles pertaining to mechanical objects (willing to try anything)

SPECIFIC SKILLS

RELATING TO COMMUNICATIONS:
Experienced and well trained in:
1. Report preparation
2. Meetings
3. Oral skills
4. Rhetorical skills
5. Overcoming barriers to communication

RELATING TO RECRUITING:
Both theoretical and practical training, knowledge, and experience
at all levels

RELATING TO SUPERVISION (INCLUDING CONTROL):
Well trained and experienced in:
1. Leadership function
2. Planning and setting desired performance goals
3. Organizing to get the job done effectively
4. Controlling on an organized basis

RELATING TO DEVELOPMENT:
Created a training and standard-operating-procedures manual totally unique in the search field.

As a result of my efforts to assist capable people in their job searches
and career development, and after much prompting, I am currently
completing a book on the techniques of carving a niche for oneself
in an organization, initially and on an ongoing basis.

Commentary
I view the above skills and abilities as assets which I have developed in
the sales and marketing fields. These skills must be viewed with the
understanding that I have progressed quite far; however, skills must, by
definition, be constantly honed and improved upon, a goal to which I am
continually committed.

PROFESSIONAL GOALS
To secure "that position"[1] with "that company"[2] which will provide me
with an excellent initial training program and the advantages of training

[1]My years of experience in this industry have taught me an important lesson:
Find a winner and make yourself indispensable! People who are always trying
to better themselves by changing jobs find that after leaving an outstanding
company like yours, the grass wasn't greener—in fact, it was artificial on top and
soiled underneath.

[2]After working in the_____industry for the last few years, I have come to the
conclusion that there is one company that I truly want to work for and one to
which I could contribute a great deal. And, most important, it is one that could
offer me a career opportunity to grow and prosper in direct relation to my efforts,
knowledge, and abilities. In short, I want your company for what I can do for it as
well as for what it can do for me.

on an ongoing basis, thereby enhancing my opportunities for personal and professional growth and success

To marry "that position" in which I can realize many of the potentials of my abilities and personality

To carve a niche for myself in a people-oriented organization which will provide myself and my family with greater opportunities for success, security, and professional growth

To be compensated on an above-average scale for doing an outstanding job

To become a truly outstanding sales, marketing, and developmental manager, known widely for my successes, knowledge, and abilities

To gain as much people, organization, and product knowledge within as short a period of time as possible so that I can contribute immediately to the growth, success, and future of that organization

PERSONAL SPECIFICS
NAME:

PLACE OF BIRTH:

DATE OF BIRTH:

AGE:

REARED IN:

CITIZENSHIP:

PHYSICAL STATISTICS: HEIGHT:

                                WEIGHT:

MARITAL STATUS:

                                DEPENDENTS:

EDUCATION: UNIVERSITY OF:

                                COLLEGE FINANCES:_____PERCENT

                                   EARNED

                                MAJORS:

                                GRADE-POINT AVERAGE

                                DEGREE

EXTRACURRICULAR ACTIVITIES:

MILITARY EXPERIENCE:

SPECIAL INTERESTS OR ABILITIES:

PROFESSIONAL EXPERIENCE:	As I indicated at the outset, I have no intention of outlining my professional experience here. This information would be on any company's application form.
INCOME REQUIREMENTS:	Open to negotiation. However, desired compensation to be based on a salary plus bonus or commission directly related to performance.
TRAVEL REQUIREMENTS:	Willing to travel nationally and internationally to a maximum of _____ percent.
REFERENCES:	Excellent personal and professional references are available to substantiate my personal and work accomplishments on request.

CREDENTIALS:

CREDO AND PHILOSOPHIES

Press on, nothing in the world can take the place of persistence. Talent will not, nothing is more common than unsuccessful men with talent. Genius will not: unrewarded genius is almost a proverb. Education alone will not, the world is full of educated derelicts. Persistence and determination alone are omnipotent.[3]

I have a low tolerance for B.S.

I am oriented toward one thing: *results*—results which are measurable.

I will be twice as demanding of myself as any employer will be.

I look upon success not as a goal but as an ongoing journey.

Luck happens when preparation meets opportunity.

My energy level is such that I never put off until tomorrow what can be accomplished today.

SHORTCOMINGS

I find that I get too involved in my work and efforts for my own good.

I want to believe that all people are as honest, hardworking, and dedicated as I am. Accordingly, I've been accused of pushing people too hard to get a job done.

[3]MacDonald Corp.

The Performance Description

This appendix contains a sample performance description. The position being described is that of outplacement consultant. It is one of four functions that were identified for several prospective employers. Each of the four functions was edited for the applicant by a close friend. The entire performance description—as finally presented—was twelve pages long. It included an introduction and conclusion and was condensed from forty-six pages.

The sample performance description is followed by an outline of what should be included in your own performance description. I suggest also that you go again to your library and review a minimum of four books dealing with types and styles of job descriptions. These should give you a lot of good ideas for broadening your performance description and getting additional exposure.

_____*Percent of time allocated to performance of this function*

THE OUTPLACEMENT CONSULTING FUNCTION

INTRODUCTION
Retaining terminated executive personnel on the payroll until they relocate is not only costly to the company but also demeaning to the people involved. In addition, they begin to feel less urgency about finding another position and are lulled into a false sense of security.

As an outplacement consultant, the recruiter can counsel decision makers on the actual termination and then help the terminated person adjust as rapidly as possible to thinking in a positive manner.

Outplacement consulting can be done on an individual and/or group basis. Each candidate can be given in-depth, individualized coaching regarding effective methods of job searching and self-placement.

BENEFITS TO BE DERIVED

In addition to saving time, effort, and money, the outplacement consultant:

1. Creates goodwill by selling the terminated executive on what this change can mean to his or her career
2. Protects the company's investment in the individual by creating the right atmosphere for rehire if this should prove desirable
3. Provides access to the company's investment in this person by utilizing industry contacts to effect a loan of the executive to companies within the industry, thereby setting the company up for reciprocal opportunities
4. Provides variety and ongoing responsibilities in the executive's life
5. Provides new challenges, prevents stagnation, and allows acquisition of new ideas and approaches to the industry
6. Provides for an appreciation of the company and the many things it does for the executive

DUTIES AND RESPONSIBILITIES

1. Assists and counsels the decision maker in the actual termination
2. Helps terminated persons adjust as rapidly as possible to thinking in a positive manner, thereby enabling them to find new positions within the industry or in another industry as quickly as possible
3. Prepares a standard-operating-procedures manual relative to the outplacement consulting function[1]

KNOWLEDGE AND SKILL EXPERIENCE REQUIREMENTS

1. Knowledge of techniques of termination which can effectively help the decision maker show the candidate that this action is in his or her interests
2. Experience in giving constructive advice on suggested techniques of termination
3. An ability to ease the transition and help the terminated employee think in a positive manner

[1]It is imperative that innovative policy-making ideas be set forth in the outplacement manual since this is a difficult area requiring the utmost tact and diplomacy. An example of this kind of policy would be providing a bonus to the terminated employee for finding a new position in a very short period of time, thereby saving the company money that would otherwise be spent in the extension of severance benefits.

4. Knowledge of, and experience with, self-placement procedures, including such aspects of the search and placement function as:
   - *a.* Problems faced in the marketplace
   - *b.* Appraisal of the marketplace itself (its fallacies)
   - *c.* Definition of the opportunities available
   - *d.* Recognition of one's skills and abilities
   - *e.* Establishing goals
   - *f.* Developing a plan of action (getting organized)
   - *g.* New methods of marketing oneself
   - *h.* Professional-profile presentations and their preparation
   - *i.* Worthwhile research materials for review
   - *j.* Techniques of interviewing
   - *k.* Appraisal of agencies and search firms
   - *l.* Avoiding the numbers game
   - *m.* Cover-letter preparation
   - *n.* Preparation of ideal-position specifications
   - *o.* Handling references
   - *p.* Salary negotiations
   - *q.* Timing and its importance
5. Overall knowledge of the industry and industry contacts, enabling the recruiter to:
   - *a.* Assist in the placement of these people within the industry
   - *b.* Use optional programs, such as lending executives to other companies
6. Effective writing skills to ensure proper preparation of the standard-operating-procedures manual
7. Knowledge gained from having been on the job market and the ability to understand and empathize with the problems encountered in the marketplace

FOLLOW-UP REQUIREMENTS

1. Reporting to the decision maker on the results of efforts in the terminated employee's behalf
2. Making periodic checks to determine the terminated employee's job-search successes
3. Reinforcing the terminated employee's positive professional and personal attitude through weekly interviews and phone calls
4. Providing additional training and direction where and when required

OUTLINE OF THE PERFORMANCE DESCRIPTION

The *introduction* should contain:

1. A short commentary referring to the company's request for additional information or your offering of this information
2. A short list of single-sentence descriptions of each major function identified

The *body* should consist of the following:
1. A short introduction for each function (one paragraph)
2. A list of benefits to be derived
3. A list of duties and responsibilities
4. A list of knowledge, skill, and experience requirements
5. A list of follow-up requirements

The *conclusion* should wrap it up nicely; it should be short, sweet, and to the point.

Success Minder and People Log

You might find the following helpful:
1. The Success Minder
2. The People Log (Figures 6 and 7)

Every day, record your long-term, intermediate-term, and short-term goals in your Success Minder. Also record the goals to be accomplished now which will allow you to achieve your short-term goals. Do this at the close of each business day; it will take only about ten minutes. You'll find that subconsciously your mind will be working, organizing, and helping you during the evening hours, preparing you for the coming day. Next day, things will move along more smoothly and in a more organized manner, and you'll accomplish much more.

In the People Log, record the names of the people you came into contact with and the date. The time and place of your meeting will be recorded in the Success Minder, not the People Log. In the code section of the People Log you record whether there is any documentation regarding this contact. For example:

CODE A—You've written a letter to this person.

CODE B—This person has written a letter to you.

CODE C—This person is extremely important to your future. You can expand on this code so that it will meet your own needs and requirements.

You might want to set up another code for other information. For example:

CODE 1—A "real person"

CODE 2—An information source

CODE 3—A competitor

Day:_____   Date:_____

SUCCESS MINDER

Long-term goal _____

Intermediate-term goal _____

Short-term goal _____

[Time] ↓	Things to do today (Immediate goals)	Phone calls	Appointments
		Other notes	

MAKE IT HAPPEN!

Fig. 6

PEOPLE LOG

Date	Code		Follow-up 1st	2nd	Action

Fig. 7

You might combine these codes in a number of different ways, setting up a complete personal profile on someone that will tell you what you want to know about this person in a matter of seconds. This is an excellent technique for recall. You can also use this code in your own address book, etc.

The action section of the People Log is self-explanatory. You should review and update it on a continuing basis.

Index